Advance praise for
Anti-Islamophobic Curriculums

"*Anti-Islamophobic Curriculums* is a thoughtful and practical book that addresses the challenges of promoting critical engagement with questions of diversity and difference in the classroom. How can teachers and students come to new understandings about why social phobias exist and find ways to challenge fear and indifference of otherness, in particular, the growing negative perceptions of Muslims and Arabs in the western world?

Rahat Zaidi's book reflects on current rhetoric around multiculturalism in Canada and poses the central question of how societies can reconstruct themselves and redefine their national identities. She suggests that societal changes can be brought about through enlightened discourse in schools underpinned by 'culturally sustaining pedagogy' that seeks to embrace literate, linguistic, and cultural pluralism within the school system. Her book offers promising examples of educational resources that address Islamophobia in meaningful ways, and can help teachers and students to confront socio-political realities in our changing world and demystify harmful stereotypes."

—*Ingrid Johnston, Professor Emerita,*
Department of Secondary Education,
University of Alberta

"*Anti-Islamophobic Curriculums* represents a major contribution to the development of educational policies and instructional practices that aim to challenge patterns of exclusion and discrimination experienced by both the Muslim community and other minoritized groups. The book affirms the power of education to shift societal attitudes and practices to challenge rather than reinforce entrenched phobic perspectives. It illustrates how this can be done by describing the development of a curriculum unit entitled *Living Together: Muslims in a Changing World* and its integration into the Alberta social studies curriculum. Timely, lucid, and instructionally important, this book should be essential reading for educators in diverse societies."

—*Jim Cummins, Professor Emeritus,*
Ontario Institute for Studies in Education,
University of Toronto

Anti-Islamophobic Curriculums

CPC
CRITICAL PRAXIS AND CURRICULUM GUIDES

Shirley R. Steinberg and Priya Parmar
Series Editors

Vol. 1

The Critical Praxis and Curriculum Guides series
is part of the Peter Lang Education list.
Every volume is peer reviewed and meets
the highest quality standards for content and production.

PETER LANG
New York • Bern • Frankfurt • Berlin
Brussels • Vienna • Oxford • Warsaw

Rahat Zaidi

Anti-Islamophobic Curriculums

PETER LANG
New York • Bern • Frankfurt • Berlin
Brussels • Vienna • Oxford • Warsaw

Library of Congress Cataloging-in-Publication Data
Names: Zaidi, Rahat, author.
Title: Anti-Islamophobic curriculums / Rahat Zaidi.
Description: New York: Peter Lang Publishing, 2017.
Series: Critical praxis and curriculum guides; vol. 1
ISSN 2166-1367 (print) | ISSN 2169-5687 (online)
Includes bibliographical references.
Identifiers: LCCN 2016045991 | ISBN 978-1-4331-2202-6 (hardcover: alk. paper)
ISBN 978-1-4331-2201-9 (paperback: alk. paper) | 978-1-4331-4255-0 (ebook pdf)
978-1-4331-4256-7 (epub) | 978-1-4331-4257-4 9 (mobi)
Subjects: LCSH: Islamophobia—Canada—Prevention.
Islam—Study and teaching—Canada.
Toleration—Study and teaching—Canada.
Multicultural education—Canada.
Classification: LCC BP43.C2 N37 2017 | DDC 305.6/97071071—dc23
LC record available at https://lccn.loc.gov/2016045991
DOI 10.3726/b11066

Bibliographic information published by **Die Deutsche Nationalbibliothek**.
Die Deutsche Nationalbibliothek lists this publication in the "Deutsche
Nationalbibliografie"; detailed bibliographic data are available
on the Internet at http://dnb.d-nb.de/.

The paper in this book meets the guidelines for permanence and durability
of the Committee on Production Guidelines for Book Longevity
of the Council of Library Resources.

© 2017 Peter Lang Publishing, Inc., New York
29 Broadway, 18th floor, New York, NY 10006
www.peterlang.com

All rights reserved.
Reprint or reproduction, even partially, in all forms such as microfilm,
xerography, microfiche, microcard, and offset strictly prohibited.

Printed in the United States of America

Contents

Foreword	vii
Preface	xi
Acknowledgments	xiii
Introduction: Anti-Islamophobic Curriculums	1

Chapter One
    Multiculturalism Policy and Practice:
    The Canadian Perspective   11

Chapter Two
    The Challenges of Multiculturalism: Canadian and
    Global Perspectives   19

Chapter Three
    Islamophobia: A Twenty-First Century Example of
    Sociophobic Development   43

Chapter Four
   Toward Culturally Sustaining Pedagogy and
   Antiphobic Initiatives   63

Chapter Five
   Foundations for an Anti-Islamophobic Curriculum   85

Conclusion   127

Foreword

As I am reading Rahat Zaidi's book and thinking about what I might write in this foreword the issues that she courageously raises in her book, expressions of Islamophobia, fear of the other and precariousness of cross-cultural understanding in a nominally multicultural society have disquietingly come to dominate the political discourse in our federal Canadian election. The issue in particular about Islamic women's rights to wear the niqab while reciting the oath for citizenship has exploded into one of the defining issues in the election campaign. Despite the Canadian Supreme Court's overturning of a government law which would make the wearing of the niqab illegal during citizen ceremonies, the Prime Minister, Stephen Harper (2006–2015), has vowed to challenge that law, and in not so coded language, has made reference to what counts as being "really" Canadian and at the same time linking the wearing of niqab to more generalized fears of terrorism. In so doing he has appealed in the basest fashion to ignorance and fear as ways to shore up his electoral support. Already, Mr. Harper's words and stance has led to violence against Muslim women, and a surge of support for his party's re-election in certain parts of the country.

Professor Zaidi notes, "writing this book has caused me to re-examine much of what I have tried to represent in my life." I take this to mean that the impetus for writing the book is not just to address immediate events as I noted above, but from a long-standing commitment to understanding how language, symbols, and cultural practices are fundamental to the education of the young. As recent events illustrate, this has becomes an even more urgent curriculum task.

While recognizing the central importance of multiculturalism in Canadian society, both as an official policy and the way that we as Canadians identify ourselves, Professor Zaidi provides signal service in reminding us that the language of multiculturalism can also lead to complacency about and assumed tolerance for cultural difference. A number of years Aoki (1996) wrote evocatively that multiculturalism can devolve into a fetish for the "things of culture." In Edmonton, where I live, there is an annual summer "Heritage Days" when literally tens of thousands of people gather to sample and experience ethnic foods, costumes, and dances. It is rightly celebrated for its peaceful display of our multicultural reality, but as Aoki notes, such events which stress "things" can ignore questions about how we really perceive and understand the other, and under what conditions and by whom, difference is tolerated.

Citing Homi Bhabha and Heidegger, Aoki stresses that culture really begins to matter at the boundaries, that is when cultures meet or to put it even more concretely, when people of different cultures meet face to face. It is at that moment when the "things of culture" do not help to craft expressions of understanding and tolerance. It is one thing to express admiration—or to recoil in fear or disgust—at expressions of cultural difference such as the niqab, but it is much more difficult to stay at the boundaries of interaction and begin the necessary conversations that understanding requires.

As Professor Zaidi writes in her reflections on multiculturalism, "perhaps the largest issue surrounding present day multiculturalism is the lack of understanding that often leads to misguided perceptions perpetuated by the media and a general lack of awareness surrounding any new culture." As she suggests this lack of understanding has become more urgent. While Canada has always been a nation of immigrants, more recent immigration from other than European countries has raised new questions, which cannot be simply contained in the passive language of multiculturalism. The recent wave of refugees from Syria and elsewhere in the Middle East and Africa has further created anxiety—and phobia—about how much "difference" a society can or should tolerate. This challenge is reflected in the questions Professor Zaidi poses for her inquiry: "How does the face of multiculturalism embrace change as it strives to integrate religious differences as well as cultural dynamics? How can cultural and religious integration succeed without isolating cultures? Should a culture be permitted to maintain its structure, to the point of segregation?"

I had the privilege of working with Professor Zaidi on other projects framed by the issues she raises in her current book. Recently, we published an edited volume focusing on hope and peace as curricular aims. In our preface we wrote,

> [...] devastating events especially strain our ability to make sense of the world. However, it is this very difficulty, that is how we develop language that begins to more generously take up a sense of the self in relation to others we recognize as a central challenge for curriculum [...] when using the term language, we are also aware that this is not just a limited notion of language in a cognitive or denotative sense, but one that involves emotional and aesthetic responses, what the political philosopher William Connolly (2013) terms "the receptive side of our engagements" (Naqvi & Smits, 2015).

Perhaps politicians feel constrained by their need to appeal to diverse communities on the one hand, and to appease specific economic, social, and cultural interests so, for example, the discourse about refugees and migrants becomes one about numbers and about protecting ourselves against possible harm and disruption. But as educators—and this to whom the book Professor Zaidi's book is most directly aimed—we cannot forego the responsibility to respond to the other in terms of our shared humanity and our distinctive and unique ways of expressing our humanity: to appeal as Connolly suggests above, to our receptive sides.

I think Professor Zaidi's book takes on this challenge admirably. She also reminds us that the imperative to educate for cultural understanding and the need to nurture our receptive sides also requires sound knowledge and forms of information that can contribute to not simply learning *about* the other, but offers language and tools for meeting at the boundaries in engaging and meaningful ways. In doing so, Professor Zaidi also reminds that such education is not simply the domain of any one subject in schools, but is something that can and should be woven into the fabric of teaching and learning across the curriculum. Professor Zaidi offers us a way of thinking about and practicing what she calls "culturally responsive teaching," a practice that challenges fear, indifference, and facile expressions of multiculturalism. Her more specific message is that we urgently require that such responsiveness take on antiphobic initiatives. It is a challenge to see the other as human, and that being human can be celebrated in expressions of diversity, not just a celebration of diversity, but an active commitment to counter fear and ignorance.

Hans Smits, University of Calgary, Canada

Hans Smits is retired from the Faculty of Education at the University of Calgary, where he served as Associate Dean of teacher preparation administering an innovative inquiry-based teacher education program. Before becoming a professor, Hans worked many years as a junior high and high school social studies teacher. He coedited two books with Rahat Naqvi entitled *Thinking About and Enacting Curriculum in "Frames of War"* (Lexington Books, 2012) and *Framing Peace: Thinking about and Enacting Curriculum as "Radical Hope"* (Peter Lang, 2015) and with Darren Lund, Lisa Panayotidis, and Jo Towers, he wrote *Provoking Conversations on Inquiry in Teacher Education* (Peter Lang, 2012).

References

Aoki, D. (1996). The thing of culture. *University of Toronto Quarterly, 65*(2), 404–418. doi:http://dx.doi.org/10.3138/utq.65.2.404

Connolly, W. E. (2013). *The fragility of things: Self-organizing processes, neoliberal fantasies, and democratic activism*. Durham: Duke University Press.

Naqvi, R., & Smits, H. (2015). *Framing peace : Thinking about and enacting curriculum as "radical hope"*. New York: Peter Lang.

Preface

It is not an easy endeavor to embrace the culture of an adopted country while at the same time honoring the culture from which one hails. The challenge to accomplish this often is accompanied by phobic reaction from the dominant culture and a general uneasiness when it comes to welcoming newcomers into a country. To be accepted into the new culture and learn to live a productive and healthy life has been the goal since patterns of immigration began taking hold. The platform of education has always been and should continue to be the primary path to achieving this. It is also the forum for provoking and questioning societal norms and a powerful means toward achieving the vision of a multicultural society living, working, and playing in harmony.

The focus of this book is to showcase a specific antiphobic curriculum to help young students become more aware of other cultures and to become acquainted with a culture beyond what has been the predominant English/French/Indigenous experience. While the emphasis of this curriculum is on the Islamic culture and the sociophobic reaction its members often encounter, the conclusions drawn are applicable to any culture.

Incorporating an antiphobic curriculum into the classroom is a positive step forward. As such, it is important to take into account the fact that the full potential of what this will accomplish can only be realized completely when the leadership from within both cultures takes an active and supportive role, both from within the host country and around the world. This demands vision and courage. With these thoughts in mind, this book is presented as one option on the journey.

Acknowledgments

On October 25, 2007, Member of Parliament for Ottawa-Vanier and Official Opposition Critic for Canadian Heritage, Francophonie and Official Languages, Hon. Mauril Bélanger presented the following motion in the House of Commons:

"That, in the opinion of the House, due to the important contributions of Canadian Muslims to Canadian Society; the cultural diversity of the Canadian Muslim community; the importance of Canadians learning about each other to foster greater social cohesion; and the important effort now underway in many Canadian communities in organizing public activities to achieve better understanding of Islamic history, the month of October should be designated Canadian Islamic History Month."

The Ottawa-Vanier MP was delighted that the House of Commons adopted this motion which highlights the important contribution of the Muslim community in Canadian society. "I encourage cultural exchanges between Canada's diverse communities, which make us a vibrant and dynamic society. I believe that by having a better understanding of our fellow Canadians from various communities and backgrounds that we will achieve a stronger and more cohesive country," said MP Bélanger.

This historic recognition marked the beginning of a series of initiatives led by the Canadian Islamic Congress. This book is the product of the support and vision in particular of one dedicated individual Professor Mohammad Elmasry, University of Waterloo, Canada. He is a Canadian engineering professor and has been a spiritual leader and visionary in the Canadian Muslim community for decades.

The curriculum was also designed with the support of the CIC and the dedicated efforts of curriculum designers Sally Goddard, Arlene Armstrong, and Sarah Soltesz. The materials have now been revised and aligned with the new program of studies in Alberta, Canada. The books can be downloaded at: www.living-together.ca.

As well I would like to acknowledge and thank the following for offering their insightful suggestions for improvement: Helen Coburn and Shea Coburn. To Shafaq Syed my sincere thanks for contributing her painting, which graces the cover of this book.

Introduction: Anti-Islamophobic Curriculums

No one is born hating another person because of the color of his skin, or his background, or his religion. People must learn to hate, and if they can learn to hate, they can be taught to love, for love comes more naturally to the human heart than it's opposite.

(Nelson Mandela, Long Walk to Freedom)

Phobia can be understood as an extreme or irrational fear of or aversion to something. Behaviors that manifest themselves within this frame often lead to societal stereotyping and predictive opinions which result in phobic reactions and mistrust amongst various social groups.

The world is currently living a prime example of social phobia. Although phobic reactions toward different cultural groups have occurred in the past this book will establish the Muslim example as demonstrative of a unique, as-of-yet unresolved concern in our society.

As a result of the "war on terrorism" certain profiling has propagated wide spread beliefs regarding the Muslim culture. In order to understand what kinds of phobia have emerged, one needs to examine the challenges that society faces today in terms of successful integration for newcomers who have belief systems different from the Anglo-Saxon Christian faith that precipitated what Canadian culture represents today. There is growing acknowledgment that the issues which such diversity brings are ever present in all sectors of life, including professional, academic, and social. These challenges are mostly characterized by the need to find a common space within which to live harmoniously and, undoubtedly, they are exacerbated by religious and cultural differences. This recognition is crucial, especially given the fact that Canada's population has a high incidence of immigrants and the world looks upon us as a champion of multiculturalism.

This manuscript, contextualized within Canada, emerges from research carried out in the field of curriculum development that builds on diversity education and antiphobic initiatives and provides an introductory framework aimed at professionals who work in a wide range of educational contexts. The author maintains that one of the most effective ways to curb negative societal reaction is by working within the school system itself.

Societal changes in attitudes are most often brought about through enlightened, learned discourse and this typically can begin in schools where society works together as educators, learners, parents, and families. The learning space is where one can have some kind of influence and impact as to how the next generations are being prepared for the future. Being "culturally responsive" is a term commonly used to define the process whereby one gains respect for diversity and religious identities. Although education boards across Canada value culturally responsive curricula, there are challenges associated with its implementation. I hope to provide a clear example of pedagogy that promotes critical engagement with issues of diversity and difference by engaging educators and learners as to why social phobias exist and how they can be minimized.

Given the current climate of hostility which has emerged as a result of global issues, it is no longer possible for us to disassociate ourselves from what is occurring in the world around us. The years following 9/11 have demonstrated how, under conditions of threat, individuals or groups can regress and develop hardened identities. They relate more with those who think like they do and with those that are recognized through social, ethnic, racial, and/or religious belief systems. Said (2001) states that even though, time has witnessed a movement toward more tolerant, inclusive behavior, the amount of hate speech and negative perceptions directed toward Muslims, and Arabs in particular, has perpetuated the paradigm of "us and them." Nevertheless, Said (2001) has pointed to the fact that, rather than portraying this as extreme clashes between cultures, society needs to acknowledge the interdependence we have on one another and reflect on its implications, especially within educational contexts. We need to determine what such interdependence in educational contexts can look like and how educators might respond to the various dimensions of space, thinking, and alternate world views. In effect, being culturally responsive is no longer a viable enough solution for what the world is witnessing. There needs to be a strategy whereby feelings of mistrust are mitigated. A community may have a concerning extremist component which influences the opinions of others toward the community as a whole. This mistrust must be assuaged by the creation of a critical awareness that includes mitigating aspects beyond stopping sociophobic reaction. These aspects include dialoguing within educational contexts and incorporating best practices. Living together requires a sense of learning together, learning from each other, and for each other (Smith, 2008). Where religion is involved we need to nurture understanding of the politicization that occurs. Without this understanding, there often occur actions that contravene the very reason for believing in a faith. As Canada's classrooms become more and more culturally and religiously diverse, education becomes the starting point for growing a society that is more aware of the people around us. Educators need to be more mindful of the facts that, more likely than not, the students in their class do not share a common belief structure. In addition, our increasingly small global context has created a window for schools to take over from talk shows and media perspectives, which are often skewed and biased. In essence, education can help our citizens better learn to discuss, with knowledge and a thoughtful, open mind, how to better live and grow within society.

To this purpose, this book has been divided into five chapters that encompass the following themes:

Multiculturalism as Policy and Practice: The Canadian Perspective

In the coming decades, demographic forces, globalization, and climate change will increase migration pressures both within and across borders. As a result, one of the most compelling challenges facing Western democracies today is how to maintain and strengthen the bonds of community across cultural lines in ever-increasing ethnically diverse societies. In much of the Western world, and particularly in Europe, there exists a widespread perception that governments are failing to meet this challenge and that they need to reconcile growing levels of multicultural diversity with a sense of a common identity (Banting, 2010).

In an effort to address this, Canada passed its Multicultural Act as a means to provide one of the most progressive approaches to immigration. Globally, Canada is regarded as a leader on the forefront of multiculturalism with other countries often looking to her as a hallmark of how best to develop multicultural policy.

As the face of immigration changes, what must be altered in policy to keep awareness of cultural shifts?

The Challenges of Multiculturalism: Canadian and Global Perspectives

Present day immigration trends present challenges to multicultural policy, in that patterns of immigration are evolving, not just within culture and race, but also within religion and tradition. Many countries are now reassessing the ability of their multicultural policies to satisfactorily maintain a sociopolitical balance between the existing culture and the new, more diverse immigrant culture permeating so much of the world now. This has resulted in often tense relations among people in countries where the rate of immigration is quickly outpacing the growth of the dominant culture and has led to governments re-examining what can be done *vis-à-vis* their immigrant and multicultural policies. A balance must be found between individuality of culture and integration of the host culture with the immigrant culture and necessitates an understanding between the two. That said, perhaps the largest issue surrounding present day multiculturalism is the lack of understanding that often leads to misguided perceptions perpetuated by the media and a general lack of awareness surrounding any new culture.

How does the face of multiculturalism embrace change as it strives to integrate religious differences as well as cultural dynamics?

How can cultural and religious integration succeed without isolating cultures?

Should a culture be permitted to maintain its structure, to the point of segregation?

Islamophobia: A Twenty-First Century Example of Sociophobic Reaction

There have been many examples of phobic reactions to new cultures throughout history. Specifically in Canada it began with the concessions of civil law, language, and religion granted by the British to the existing French population in Canada by the Quebec Act of 1774. These concessions were the direct result of the fear the British had that the French Canadians would join the American Revolutionaries and England would lose its toehold in North America entirely. The Irish immigrants, the "temporary" Chinese workers, and the Japanese internment all provided other examples of cultures hard hit by peoples' ignorance. In the twenty-first century, the most relevant current example of phobic reaction is that of "Islamophobia." This phenomenon has grown exponentially since September 11, 2001. Many people have been led to accept stereotypes about Islamic culture due largely to generalized interpretations of behavior and dogma of an extremist faction of Islam.

Although contested, islamophobia has come to refer to both anti-Muslim (group of people) and anti-Islam (the religion) sentiments. These may overlap with racism, xenophobia, antireligious, and anti-immigrant views as well (Cesari, 2011, p. 24). Islamophobia was further brought to the forefront by Kofi Anan, Secretary General of the United Nations in 2004, who addressed it at a UN conference in 2004 titled "Confronting Islamophobia: Education for Tolerance and Understanding" (United Nations, 2014). Anan summed up his comments as follows: "When the world is compelled to coin a new term to take account of increasingly widespread bigotry—that is a sad and troubling development. Such is the case with Islamophobia" (United Nations, 2014, para. 3).

How can sentiments of Islamophobia be countered successfully so as to reduce tension and increase cultural integration?

Culturally Responsive Teaching and Examples of Antiphobic Initiatives

One of the more subtle, but also very effective, means by which to enlighten the general population about Islam and other topics of social phobia is through effective education, especially at the primary level. By specifically examining the present curriculum at the level of K–9 education, teachers, and curriculum leaders can develop more effective methods of covering topics related to immigration and, particularly, cultural contributions by minority groups.

Antiphobic initiatives are necessary to increase awareness of societal contributions by minority groups. For example, once each culture has a better understanding of the origins, contributions, and traditions of the other, one can theorize that phobia will decrease, and curiosity will arise, furthering exploratory information-seeking, often facilitated by the education system.

What are some of the benefits of introducing an antiphobic curriculum?

Foundations for an Anti-Islamophobic Curriculum

Smith (2008) reiterated the importance of being able to access basic religious information that is both direct and unassuming. The curriculum introduced in this book is presented to K–9 students in a simple and nonconversionary manner. In Smith's words, it is friendly, giving the opportunity for young, non-Muslims to better understand their Muslim friends and neighbors.

Placing integrated learning structures that incorporate information about new cultures into a curriculum, not only informs about physical contributions, but also connects customs and traditions with the mainstream culture. In order to counteract the pervasive generalizations of social, journalistic, and critical media, it is necessary that people are provided from a young age, with enough information to make educated decisions about how they will react to new and ever-changing cultural dynamics within their own country.

Is it possible to revise curriculum as a contributing force in decreasing social phobia?

So What Now? What's Next? Where Do We Go From Here?

Writing this book has caused me to re-examine much of what I have tried to represent in my life. I see that the world has changed so very much since this project began. Society is no longer using 9/11 as the starting point to talk about sociophobia. Events in the world have progressed to other issues now, including what to do about ISIS, the Islamist terrorist organization using very high-tech means to recruit young men and women, suffering from inertia, rudderless, and feeling displaced with no direction in their lives. Often they are immigrants themselves in a new country, who have no feelings of support from their new government or culture. Some are even citizens of their country of origin. They have become what is called radicalized, used for the purposes of the organization that has recruited them, some becoming human bombs and forced into opposing thinking patterns.

My hope is that, by starting at the base level of meeting young people at a common place where they all come together on a regular basis (school), society can use education as the catalyst to help dispel some of the myths and fears and also engage our young people in open, honest dialogue.

Background

I have spent the last ten years conducting research in highly ethnically diverse schools in Canada, during which I have been disturbed by the strong dichotomies that are embedded in social norms around the good and the bad, the right and the wrong, and the progressive West and the Others. These discourses have been made apparent through impoverished versions of culture where questioning such realities is a sign of not belonging. My work has been contextualized in the notion of difference and how it is lived in schools and often goes unnoticed.

I have sought to create collaborative, inspirational, and critical learning opportunities that can engage teachers and students alike in working toward a collective notion of being.

One aspect that has become apparent to me is the importance of targeting mainstream educational institutions and engaging in critical conversations with teachers about difference. The work as identified by Anan is a challenging and complicated endeavor that requires active participation within educational systems. In other words, schools and, more broadly, teacher educators need to be made aware of their global, plural, and often intercultural identities (United Nations, 2014). It is only through systemic awareness and intentional work that we can move away from phobic reactions toward specific communities and ethnicities. I have also learned through my interactions that, despite the fact that the twenty-first century is young, we face a complex and serious situation that needs to be attended to. Education plays one key role in the process as it paves the way for a future that can help us foster a more positive societal attitude toward difference.

We are a society that has a shared responsibility not only for ourselves, but also for the ethics that sustain a culture created through difference (Chambers, 1990, p. 115). This line of reasoning has important implications for community empowerment, especially within multiethnic and multiracial societies. Educators need to engage practically with innovative philosophical underpinnings that, when solidified, will enable successful implementation of ideas and rejuvenated education systems. The importance of achieving this has been summarized by Giroux (1992) who advises:

> Educating for difference, democracy, and ethical responsibility is not about creating passive citizens. It is about providing students with the knowledge, capacities, and opportunities to be noisy, irreverent, and vibrant. Central to this concern is the need for students to understand how cultural, ethnic, racial, and ideological differences enhance the possibility for dialogue, trust, and solidarity. Given this perspective, difference can be analyzed and constructed within pedagogical contexts that promote compassion and tolerance rather than envy, hatred, and bigotry (p. 8).

In essence, what Giroux is advocating is that today's students need not be subjected to a totalized view of culture, literacy, and citizenship. They deserve ideas which prepare them to identify with a system that nurtures their intellect while at the same time provides them the ability to have a reflexive relationship with it.

Adams (2012) wrote about present-day examples in our society that further amplify the need for a deeper understanding of difference. His examples were drawn from current conflicts emerging in Western culture. Marois' (LeBlanc, 2013) proposed (and later defeated) secular charter that would restrict hijabs while tolerating crucifixes fell into a range of phobic reactions in the West against the Muslim tide of immigration, which run from the truly atrocious to the merely vexatious (LeBlanc, 2013).

Anders Breivik was convicted of murdering seventy-seven people in pursuit of his crusade against multiculturalism. In New York City, a court has ordered the transit system to accept an advertisement that describes Arabs as "savages" (Mackey, 2012, para. 1). In recent years here in Canada, there has existed controversy about whether veiled Muslim women should be allowed to vote, despite the lack of evidence that this has ever been a source of election fraud" (Adams, 2012). As this book was being written, new examples have emerged almost weekly. These examples strike a familiar chord with us, reminding us that we are surrounded on a daily basis by controversies around the limits of multiculturalism. Even in 2015, the challenge still remains as to how society can learn to relate to its members in a respectful, constructive manner. This leaves us with many questions still to be answered:

What does it mean to be respectful of diversity?

Can we engage in a collective project of nation building framed within the policies of multiculturalism?

What would such a project entail?

Is it true that in accepting immigrants into Canada and allowing them to keep facets of their former identity alive we are sleep walking our way to segregation (Phillips, 2005)?

Are certain groups or ethnicities viewed as threats to such collective nation building?

What is it about "them" that fosters fear? Or is this more a question of ignorance?

References

Adams, P. (August 27, 2012). Is Stephen Harper saving us from Islamophobia? Retrieved from http://ipolitics.ca/2012/08/27/paul-adams-is-stephen-harper-saving-us-from-islamophobia/

Banting, K. G. (2010). Is there a progressive's dilemma in Canada? Immigration, multiculturalism and welfare state: Presidential address to the Canadian political science association. *Canadian Journal of Political Science, 43*(4), 797–820.

Cesari, J. (2011). Islamophobia in the West: A comparison between Europe and the United States. In Esposito, J., & Kalin, I. (Eds.), *Islamophobia: The challenge of pluralism in the 21st century* (pp. 21–43). New York, NY: Oxford University Press.

Chambers, I. (1990). *Border dialogues: Journeys in postmodernity*. London: Routledge.

Giroux, H. A. (1992). *Border crossings: Cultural workers and the politics of education*. New York; London: Routledge.

LeBlanc, D. (September 6, 2013). Marois blasts multiculturalism in defence of 'values' charter. *The Globe and Mail*. Retrieved from http://www.theglobeandmail.com/news/politics/marois-blasts-multiculturalism-promises-gradual-phase-in-of-quebec-secular-values-charter/article14158590/

Mackey, R. (2012, August 21). Anti-Islam ads remixed in San Francisco and New York. *The Lede: The New York Times News Blog*. Retrieved from http://thelede.blogs.nytimes.com/2012/08/21/anti-islam-ads-remixed-in-san-francisco-and-new-york/?_r=2 - more-186629

Mandela, N. (1994). *Long walk to freedom: The autobiography of Nelson Mandela* (1st ed.). Boston: Little, Brown.

Phillips, T. (2005). *After 7/7: Sleepwalking to segregation*.

Said, E. (2001). The clash of ignorance. *The Nation, 273*(12), 11–13.

Smith, D. G. (2008). Preface: Living together, learning together. http://www.living-together.ca/pdfs/teachersguide.pdf

United Nations. (December 7, 2014). Secretary-General, addressing headquarters seminar on confronting Islamophobia, stresses importance of leadership, two-way integration, dialogue. Retrieved from http://www.un.org/press/en/2004/sgsm9637.doc.htm

Chapter I

Multiculturalism Policy and Practice: The Canadian Perspective

It was 1950 when Hendrick and his wife Nicola emigrated from the Netherlands with their two young sons. They set up their new lives in Edmonton, Alberta, Hendrick beginning a job in the steel industry, picking up where he had left off in the Netherlands. The neighborhood they eventually settled in was home to a variety of families, all beginning lives as immigrants in their new, post-Second World War environs. The majority came from all over Western Europe; from Scotland and the British Isles, Italy and France, Portugal and the Netherlands, Germany and Yugoslavia. Multiculturalism was taking a foothold in Canada.

Multiculturalism can refer to a demographic detail, a particular set of philosophical ideas, or a specific positioning by government or institutions toward a diverse population. By definition, advocates of multiculturalism generally scorn the idea of a single homogenous culture and, instead, extol a society promoting a range of lifestyles, philosophies, religions, practices, and codes (Gay, 1994). Likewise, there is reluctance on their part to accept the superiority of one culture over another, and, in fact, key to (Canadian) multiculturalism, is the fundamental belief that all citizens are equal, can maintain their identities, take pride in their ancestry, and have a sense of belonging within the larger society. In short, they believe that cultural diversity enriches a society.

Multiculturalism's Historical Perspective

Canada, like the other major British-settled societies (the US, Australia, and New Zealand), initially adopted an assimilationist approach to immigration (Palmer, 2002). In 1869, when the federal government passed the first Immigration Act, the basic framework of Canadian immigration policy was established (Makarenko, 2010). An open door policy encouraged immigrants to come to Canada with very few restrictions, with the exception of criminals, and assimilate to the pre-existing British mainstream culture, with the hope that, over time, they would become generally indistinguishable from native-born British, perhaps English-speaking Canadians in their speech, dress, recreation, and way of life. And they did. Canada was seen as a destination for migration. The initial focus of the government's policy was primarily to attract farmers and laborers, preferably Caucasian, and discouraged urban workers, artisans, and tradesmen (Makarenko, 2010).

After the First World War, multiculturalism was still encouraged and immigration continued; however, those coming from nations such as Germany, Austria, and Hungary were recognized as enemy aliens under the War Measures Act, 1914 (Makarenko, 2010). The fear of communism and other ideologies prohibited certain groups such as the Dukhobors and Mennonites from entering the country as well.

During the post-Second World War years Canada's view of multiculturalism began to change again and immigration was looked upon as a means to increase its economic power. A new act was created that differentiated "preferred" classes of immigrants, including those who were British subjects, and citizens of France and the United States. Those of Asian descent were discriminated against immigrating unless they already had relatives in Canada. Also discriminated against were homosexuals and those people with mental disabilities (Makarenko, 2010). As a result, large-scale migration successfully shifted sizable proportions of populations bounded by commonalities such as religion, ethnicity, and culture in areas where these groups traditionally did not have an ancestral claim.

It was during the 1970s that Canada's perceived value of multiculturalism was particularly pronounced. A unique set of policies has characterized Canada's global stance toward immigrants and diversity and these were shaped by the Canadian Government's Multiculturalism Policy introduced in 1971 under then Prime Minister Pierre Elliott Trudeau (Library and Archives Canada, 1971). The policy became enshrined as an Act of Parliament in 1988 under Prime Minister Brian Mulroney's leadership. Canada was the first country to adopt this type of legislation as an official act and, in so doing, affirmed the value and dignity of all Canadian citizens regardless of their racial or ethnic origins, their language, or their religious affiliation. In addition, one of the principal objectives of the 1971 Multiculturalism Policy of Canada was to entrench the rights of Aboriginal peoples and the status of Canada's two official languages.

Canada's Multicultural Act has given Canadians a feeling of security and self-confidence, making them more open to, and accepting of, diverse culture; at least in theory. The Act has demonstrated that multiculturalism encourages racial and ethnic harmony and cross-cultural understanding. As a result, the Canadian government has gained a global reputation as a world leader in implementing multicultural policy.

Kobayashi (1993) has identified different stages of the development of multiculturalism in Canada. The first is connected to demographic realities and acknowledges that English and French charter groups are not the sole representatives of Canada's landscape. Historically, this acknowledgment was manifested in the lobbying of other Canadians to the Bilingualism and Biculturalism Commission and the inclusion of their call for cultural pluralism.

The official declaration of multiculturalism in 1971 signaled the second stage in the growth of this policy that Kobayashi (1993) describes as symbolic multiculturalism. This was characterized by an unfocussed support and celebration of cultural diversity through ethnic organizations and cultural centers that included the promotion of ethnically diverse foods, art, music, and dance, all markers of a type of multiculturalism, simplistic in nature that was promoted, and generally embraced, within Canadian society. In fact, Bissoondath (1994) stated cultural differences were promoted under this model and ethnic groups were encouraged to preserve these cultural dissimilarities and values. In many ways, this is the most common representation of Canadian multiculturalism.

In the third period (2004–2005), multiculturalism was characterized by the advancement of human rights as constitutionally protected in the Canadian Charter of Rights and Freedoms (Kobayashi, 1993). Ley (2010) describes the evolution and growth of Canada's multicultural policy and further expands, pointing out that it was during this period the Canadian Government published the annual report on the Multiculturalism Act. It identified four priority areas that needed further development and improvement. These were described as follows:

(1) Fostering cross-cultural understanding,
(2) Combating racism,
(3) Promoting civic participation, and
(4) Making Canadian institutions more reflective of Canadian diversity.

In short, an emphasis was placed on supporting programs and initiatives that would facilitate an understanding of cross-cultural differences, combat racism, and engage cultural communities in greater civic participation. In a more recent update in 2012, the Government of Canada—Federal Department of Canadian Heritage—described the official policy of multiculturalism as follows:

> Canadian multiculturalism is fundamental to our belief that all citizens are equal. Multiculturalism ensures that all citizens can keep their identities, can take pride in their ancestry and have a sense of belonging. Acceptance gives Canadians a feeling of security and self-confidence, making them more open to, and accepting of, diverse cultures. The Canadian experience has shown that multiculturalism encourages racial and ethnic harmony and cross-cultural understanding, and discourages ghettoization, hatred, discrimination and violence (para. 2).

Problematizing Multiculturalism

Since the introduction of the multicultural policy, the Canadian landscape has changed somewhat dramatically. Current data released by Statistics Canada (2011) highlight the growing linguistic, cultural, and religious diversity across the country. Unlike previous waves of immigrants coming to Canada, twenty-first century immigrants are more apparent, sporting more diverse religious, ethnic, linguistic, and physical characteristics, which set them apart from previous European immigrants. In fact, much more emphasis is placed now on an immigrant's religion, this coming on the heels of Canada's most recent immigration pattern branded by a unique set of characteristics. In fact, a key need that has been identified within the Canadian context, and in many ways echoes what other world governments are saying, is to articulate clear policies that, in particular, deal with religious identities.

Reports in Canada compiled by the multicultural sector acknowledge the significant growing religious diversity within the country and there is general consensus around the fact that the place of religious diversity within multiculturalism has not yet been adequately debated nor explored (Kymlicka, 2007, 2008). Kymlicka (2010), in his report on the current state of multiculturalism in Canada, points to the increasingly important role religion plays. As specific examples, he makes references to the heated debates on religious family law arbitration, the funding of religious schools in Ontario, and the reasonable accommodation debate in Quebec. As well, he underlines how religion is becoming the most controversial aspect of multiculturalism.

In 2008, Gerard Bouchard and Charles Taylor released a report as Co-chairs of the Consultation Commission on Accommodation Practices Related to Cultural Differences. The Commission was set up by the Quebec government in response to public discontent concerning "reasonable accommodation" of religious and cultural practices. In the report, four delicate issues, among others, were examined: cultural integration, collective identity, church-state relations, and the most appropriate procedures for handling cultural and religious harmonization requests.

The Bouchard-Taylor (2008) report is perhaps the first sustained public report on the topic of multiculturalism in Canada, and, although focused on Quebec, its analysis is relevant, both on national and international levels. The report maintains that, although the existing constitutional and legislative framework of "reasonable accommodation" and "open secularism" in Canada has merit, it is necessary to do more work to help front-line workers and officials who deal regularly with the task of actually implementing the policy and managing the debate it raises. It is within this context that the problematization of multiculturalism is most obvious. Peritz & Friesen (2010) state:

> Though there is widespread enthusiasm for the idea of multiculturalism, its reality remains complex and at times volatile. Consider that every four years Canada accepts a million newcomers. Within two decades, nearly 30 per cent of the population will be foreign-born. Increasingly, newcomers to Canada earn less than previous generations of immigrants. Their Canadian-born children, although they typically excel in school, are, according to one study, less likely to feel a sense of belonging in Canada (para. 4).

These tendencies occurring quite frequently late into 2014 have spurred what has come to be called "radicalization" movements (Royal Canadian Mounted Police, 2011; Wilner & Dubouloz, 2010). The term "radicalization" is a relatively new societal term derived from the word radical, defined by Merriam Webster dictionary as "having extreme political or social views that are not shared by most people." The word spurs controversy around questions of successful integration into mainstream society. Whether the proposed law to ban niqabs in Quebec or the recent issue of whether or not to allow the hijab or burka to be permitted to be worn in a citizenship ceremony, or the murdering of a military guard in Ottawa, all relate to the question of religious accommodation and the challenges now facing Canada's multicultural policy.

Through its evolution, the concept of multiculturalism has now come to a point where religion and religious diversity are playing a more important role in the spectrum. The immigrant must go beyond just surviving and living in mainstream society and must ask him/herself how he/she can live, grow, and prosper, for example, as a Jewish Canadian or a Muslim Canadian or a Sikh Canadian. Although the school system has stepped in to help answer these questions, gaps still exist, especially in light of world politics as they relate to the immigrant situation today. There are new forces at play in the twenty-first century and new questions have surfaced:

- Is it possible to live up to the expectations of the Multicultural Act?
- How can we encourage and grow a multicultural society within a culture of fear and distrust of "the other"?

Canada's Multicultural Act, for many years, has been, at least in theory, an act with a goal of providing security and self-confidence to a nation still young and in need of self-identification. It has provided a means for a country to be open and accepting of cultural diversity. Nonetheless, the changes that have occurred through Canada's short history have prompted many to re-examine how today's immigrant (different in appearance and religion from his/her historical counterparts) in an already diverse Canada can live up to the Act's expectations. Governments are questioning how we can continue to live and grow as a productive society and whether or not the Multicultural Act needs tweaking or even discarding.

Canada's Multicultural Act has attempted to sort out the intricacies of immigration and lead the country to a place where we can all live together in harmony. As new waves of immigrants come to Canada, it is becoming apparent, however, that the clauses in the Act are not sufficient to address the complexities faced by newcomers. Many governments now feel the whole concept of living out the tenets of any of the multicultural acts now in place seem to be overpowered by more and different sociopolitical stressors that have superseded the somewhat idealistic vision of all groups, faith, and cultures living together in harmony.

References

Bissoondath, N. (1994). *Selling illusions: the cult of multiculturalism in Canada*. London: Penguin Books.

Bouchard, G., & Taylor, C. (2008). Building the future: A time for reconciliation. Retrieved from https://www.mce.gouv.qc.ca/publications/CCPARDC/rapport-final-integral-en.pdf

Gay, G. (1994). A synthesis of scholarship in multicultural education. http://www.ncrel.org/sdrs/areas/issues/educatrs/leadrshp/le0gay.htm

Kobayashi, A. (1993). Multiculturalism: Representing a Canadian institution *Place, culture and representation* (pp. 205–231). London: Routledge.

Kymlicka, W. (2007). Ethnocultural diversity in a liberal state: Making sense of the Canadian model(s). In Banting, K. G., Courchene, T., Seidle, T. J., & Leslie, F. (Eds.). *Belonging?: Diversity, recognition and shared citizenship in Canada, 3*, 39–86.

Kymlicka, W. (2008). The three lives of multiculturalism [Lecture]. http://www.acade mia.edu/2397536/The_Three_Lives_of_Multiculturalism_2008_

Kymlicka, W. (2010). The rise and fall of multiculturalism? New debates on inclusion and accommodation in diverse societies. In Vertovec S., & Wessendorf, S. (Eds.), *The multiculturalism backlash: European discourses, policies and practices* (pp. 190–206). New York, NY: Routledge.

Ley, D. (2010). Multiculturalism: A Canadian defence. In S. Vertovec & S. Wessendorf (Eds.), *The multiculturalism backlash: European discourses, policies and practices* (pp. 190–206). New York, NY: Routledge.

Library and Archives Canada. (October 8, 1971). Canadian Multiculturalism Policy, 1971. Retrieved from from http://www.pier21.ca/research/immigration-history/canadian-multiculturalism-policy-1971

Makarenko, J. (2010). Immigration policy in Canada: History, administration, and debates. Mapleleafweb http://mapleleafweb.com/features/immigration-policy-canada-history-administration-and-debates - historyerence

Palmer, H. (2002). Reluctant hosts: Anglo-Canadian views of multiculturalism in the twentieth century. In Francis, R. D. & Smith, D. B. (Eds.), *Readings in Canadian history: Post confederation* (pp. 116–130). Toronto, ON: Nelson.

Peritz, I., & Friesen, J. (2010). Part 1: When multiculturalism doesn't work. *The Globe and Mail*. Retrieved from http://www.theglobeandmail.com/news/national/time-to-lead/part-1-when-multiculturalism-doesnt-work/article1318798/

Royal Canadian Mounted Police. (June 7, 2011). Youth online and at risk: Radicalization facilitated by the internet. Retrieved from http://www.rcmp-grc.gc.ca/nsci-ecsn/rad/rad-eng.htm - rad

Statistics Canada. (2011). 2011 National household survey: Immigration, place of birth, citizenship, ethnic origin, visible minorities, language and religion. http://www.statcan.gc.ca/daily-quotidien/130508/dq130508b-eng.htm

Wilner, A., & Dubouloz, C.-J. (2010). Homegrown terrorism and transformative learning: An interdisciplinary approach to understanding radicalization. *Global Change, Peace, & Security, 22*(1), 35–51.

Chapter II

The Challenges of Multiculturalism: Canadian and Global Perspectives

During Canada's first national internment operations of 1914–20, a total of 8759 men, accompanied by some women and children, were confined in twenty-four 'concentration camps' spread across the Dominion. Among the internees, some 6000 were civilians, officially described as 'Austro-Hungarians' of whom the majority, approximately 5000 men, women, and children, were probably Ukrainians by nationality, most of them recent immigrants, although some were naturalized British subjects, Canadian-born. Interned alongside them were genuine German and Austrian POWs but also others of 'Austro-Hungarian nationality,' including Poles, Italians, Bulgarians, Rumanians, Turks, Jews, Croatians, and Serbians.

(Luciuk, 2000, p. 17)

Multiculturalism has borne the brunt of a renewed round of challenges this decade, more significant because they are now populist, politicized and widely publicized reactions to traumatic events. Indeed much contemporary popular writing is inspired by the cross-national transmission of media text and images that selectively highlight points of crisis, presenting them as normative, eliding significant differences in national conditions, and sliding across thin ice in prescribing causality. In this spontaneous and often uncritical transmission of tarnished ethnoscapes from elsewhere, multiculturalism has been projected as the abiding context, the grab bag for all manner of policy failures.

(Ley, 2010, p. 198)

Canada's Multicultural Act represents an example of providing effective policy and legislation through which immigrants are given the opportunity to preserve their language, culture, and religious beliefs. It is an empowering act, providing a space to honor one's culture of origin while fostering and nurturing a new identity in the adopted homeland. Canada today is defined as a multicultural society precisely because of, *and* in spite of, the persistence and uniquely characterized behaviors of all the immigrant groups that have stepped onto her shores. As future generations were born and filled Canadian schools, workplaces, and cities, Canada's Multicultural Act was often perceived as a forward-thinking way of showing the world how it "could be done." The Act has been lauded, hated, celebrated, and ridiculed, yet emulated (to different levels of success) since its inception.

Inasmuch as the policy's objectives are honorable in their intent, the philosophy behind them has not been without controversy or debate. In addition to issues of successful economic and social integration of immigrants, policy makers and officials face the challenge of how to foster both meaningful civic engagement and global citizenship within the immigrant community. Each of these challenges has helped enhance immigrant identities and, on the flip side, has also represented difficult ideals to realize as policy makers grapple with incidents of racism and marginalization *vis-à-vis* minority groups. Transitioning into the dominant society is never easy and, in some cases, never happens.

Immigrants have always faced challenges with respect to linguistic, cultural, educational, and religious inclusion and these factors are further amplified by societal perceptions around the complex identities people typically demonstrate when they enter a new cultural milieu. In addition, a common thread, dominant in most historical narratives, is the perception that newcomers are a threat to mainstream society because of one or another belief structure, behavior, or action. This book recognizes the struggles and sociopolitical issues that have historically emerged when different cultures were being asked to live together in harmony. It highlights the stories of marginalization and challenges around successful integration of newcomers into mainstream society that remain fairly similar, both in content as well as context.

Throughout history, immigrants have survived within their groups, seeking like-minded people with whom they worked and socialized. Kymlicka (2010) notes that "multiculturalism is as old as humanity" (p. 35). Different cultures have always found ways of coexisting, and respect for diversity was a familiar icon of many historic empires. The history of a country like Canada, for example, has been marked by a variety of immigrant groups: the early phase of French immigration in the late sixteenth and early seventeenth centuries followed by immigration from Great Britain during the mid eighteenth century. The influx of the Loyalist population after the American War of Independence greatly increased the number and influence of English speaking inhabitants. Irish immigrants who began arriving between 1825 and 1970 and the first Jewish people immigrated to Canada in the 1750s. By 1867, the Irish were the second largest ethnic group after the French (Carrothers, 1948).

Other parts of the world experienced similar immigration patterns. In Britain, for example, after 1945 there were three main sets of arrivals: refugees from Europe displaced by war such as the Cold War (e.g., Poles, Hungarians) migrant workers and their families, especially from Southern Europe (e.g., Italians), and Empire/Commonwealth immigrants from the Caribbean and South Asia (Fryer, 2010; Rose & Associates, 1969; Runnymede, 2000; Watson, 1977). The first flow of immigrants to the Netherlands consisted of inhabitants of the former Dutch East Indies, who arrived after the independence of Indonesia in 1949. During the 1950s and 1960s, they were joined by guest workers from Mediterranean countries, particularly Yugoslavia, Morocco, and Turkey (Prins & Saharso, 2009). Australia's population history was initially characterized by the Indigenous peoples and later on, between 1940 and 1970, by immigration from Northern Europe, Southern Europe, and South Asia (Foster & Stockley, 1988).

All this to say that the rhetoric around immigration was fairly consistent worldwide and marked by a plethora of different reactions, from economic acceptance, to political strategy that said this was good for the country, to a general distrust. This distrust was exemplified in Blanshard's (1984) book in which he raised the alarm over the flood of Roman Catholic immigrants to the United States. He described them as a threat to democracy, equality, and secular values, emphasizing that they came from countries that were almost all authoritarian, religiously fundamentalist, and opposed to the rights of women and the practice of birth control. He further stated that Catholics could not and would not be integrated. His book was a best seller for eleven months on the New York Times list.

Both the Irish and the Jewish faced discrimination from mainstream society and as a result, developed strong insular communities. These two groups were often viewed as being extremist in their religious beliefs and practices and perceived as a threat to democracy and mainstream society.

In contrast, Fujiwara (2012) discusses how the Scottish in Canada were perceived as less threatening to mainstream society because, "the Scots helped to define what mainstream Canada should be, having a huge impact on its political, educational, and economic development and philosophical underpinnings as members of the dominant British group" (p. 6). Other immigrant minorities such as the Ukrainians are discussed in Fujiwara's work in which he analyses how their old world political ideologies and involvement were never accepted by mainstream Canadians before the Second World War. It was only after the war they were "more or less acknowledged for their economic contribution as prairie farmers and allowed naturalization and the franchise (Fujiwara, 2012, p. 8)." He further outlines how the dividing line from mainstream Canada, with the exception of a small number who did not settle in British Columbia, was the most significant for immigrants of Japanese descent because of the physical uniqueness of their race and non-Christian culture and traditions. In fact, the Japanese were denied the franchise until 1948 and they were under the close influence of the Japanese consulates until the Second World War (Fujiwara, 2012, p. 6).

The government also suspended their human rights when they were moved to internment camps during the Second World War as a result of an increased phobia toward all Japanese after the bombing of Pearl Harbor. From 1885–1923, Chinese families and their descendants were also targeted, obligated to pay a head tax, intended to block their immigration. This law was followed by a ban on Chinese immigration until 1947.

Presently, issues around multiculturalism have also emerged on a global level as the world has witnessed the increasing animosity, anxiety, and hostility expressed toward specific cultural groups advocating extremist (religious) views and the challenges continue to expand and evolve with the global situation.

Gregg (2006) and Fulford (2006) note that the stakes have indeed been raised. It is not just separation and difference that are now the popular causes of concern, but rather *hostile difference*. Introverted communities are characterized by social separation and economic marginality that aid receptiveness to ideologies and projects that challenge, and, in a few instances, violently challenge, national values and civic order. It is multiculturalism, we are told, that has encouraged cultural difference, social isolation, the perpetuation, and even the perversion of homeland beliefs and disloyalty to the new state. In fact, during the twenty-first century and especially as a result of these perceptions, this attitude has become very much a part of the discourse surrounding justification for the general retreat from multiculturalist policies, particularly in countries such as the Netherlands, the United Kingdom, and Australia. It is hence worthwhile to examine the nature of the arguments given in favor of this general retreat and it is also important to take note of particular ethnic groups that emerge as central in this discussion.

The example of the Netherlands is highlighted repeatedly by critics as the object lesson of the failure of multiculturalism. Muslim immigrants who have landed on Dutch soil and have begun taking up a prominent place within the Dutch culture have taken the brunt of this criticism. In 2000, a Netherlands journalist, Paul Scheffer, published an article entitled *The Multicultural Drama* (Scheffer, 2000), followed by a book entitled *Immigrant Nations: Achieving Consensus on the Politics of Multiculturalism* (Scheffer, 2011). During this time, the Netherlands' history was marked by a series of incidents such as the death of the film-maker Theodoor Van Gogh who produced the short film *Submission* in 2004, in which he criticized the treatment of Muslim women. Many Muslims found it controversial and on November 2, 2004 Van Gogh was assassinated by Mohammed Bouyeri, a Dutch-Moroccan Muslim. Hurewitz (2005) later suggested:

> The Netherlands, as are many other European countries, is grappling with a perceived failed assimilation of its post-World War II (Muslim) immigrants. France, Germany, Belgium and other countries have experienced similar incidents highlighting the Muslim extremist threat, and no one doubts that radicals are operating across the continent. But the Netherlands—with the assassination first of right-wing politician Pim Fortuyn and more recently of van Gogh—has become a flashpoint for the conflict of Muslim and Western society (para. 7).

In October 2010, controversy erupted amid Thilo Sarrazin's best-selling book *Deutschland Schafft Sich Ab* (Germany is Abolishing Itself). In his book, Sarrazin denounced the policy on post-World War II immigration that Germany had created. The book sparked international debate regarding policies and practices of multiculturalism, evoking political commentary from both German Chancellor Angela Merkel and British Prime Minister Dave Cameron, who both declared that multiculturalism had failed in their countries (Burns, 2011). After examining their respective countries' multiculturalism practices, both leaders agreed that their policies had not lived up to their expectations. They both outlined the extreme difficulty of trying to nurture models of citizenship among different ethnic cultural groups that did not fit into the mold of the mainstream national. These groups, according to Merkel and Cameron, looked different, spoke a different language, and worshipped a different God, all factors deemed dangerously significant in creating mistrust and agitation (including sociophobic reaction) toward a specific culture (Burns, 2011).

In 2011, Anders Behring Breivik, a thirty-three-year-old Norwegian, murdered seventy-seven people in two attacks under the guise that he was at war against multiculturalism. He was subsequently charged with committing acts of terror and in 2012 he indicated to the Norwegian court that the children and teens he killed were legitimate targets because they were political activists who choose to fight for multiculturalism. Breivik was not alone in his paranoia toward immigrants and outsiders. Such attitudes are being shaped by demographic shifts occurring all over the world, especially in Western Europe and North America, whose society is feeling the impact on all levels. Saunders (2012) reminds us that "the arrival of millions of people from poor religious-minority backgrounds in Western countries was a traumatic, politically controversial, sometimes violent affair that occupied front pages and stood at the forefront of our political consciousness for the better part of two generations" (p. 114).

The twenty-first century is presenting Canada with new challenges of a different nature in that, as previously stated, it is now also a country defined by a diversity that is different from the historical trajectory witnessed in previous decades. In fact, events unfolding on the eve of the twenty-first century would become a harbinger of what was to transpire well into the first decade of the year 2000. In the 1990s, as the leader of the militant group al-Qaida, Osama bin Laden declared war on the United States and was behind the attacks on the United States, America's embassies in Kenya and Tanzania, the World Trade Center, and the Pentagon as well as the attacks in London, Madrid, Bali, and beyond (Maraia, 2011). The capture of Bin Ladin in 2011 marked a decisive turning point in what the world was calling the war on terrorism. In May 2011, following Bin Ladin's death, Colonel John Maraia from the United States Institute of Peace offered the following thoughts: *"Osama bin Laden's killing by U.S. forces is a significant symbolic victory in America's ongoing counter-terrorism campaign. After 9/11, President George W. Bush declared that the U.S. would bring bin Laden to justice, dead or alive... Killing the acknowledged leader of al-Qaida is a critical step in this war of ideas and images; it clearly sends the message to bin Laden's followers that America's pursuit is relentless [...]"* (Maraia, 2011, para. 1). As much as Bin Ladin's death generated a symbolic satisfaction and a hope that in death, the terrorism movement would no longer exist, the world continued to be witness to increasing jihadist movements.

Two decades into the twenty-first century, the rise of another extreme militant group known as ISIS (the Islamic State of Iraq and Syria) has ignited further fears of what President Barack Obama (2009–2017) has called a "network of death." ISIS became a major force very quickly and the United States, along with coalition forces, has been fighting a new war in Iraq and Syria. To iterate an example, just before noon on Wednesday January 7, 2015, two masked men armed with automatic rifles entered the offices of the weekly satirical newspaper *Charlie Hebdo* in central Paris and gunned down newspaper staff and police officers, killing twelve and wounding many more. Several more innocent people would die in subsequent days before the two gunmen and an accomplice, who took hostages in a Jewish supermarket, were killed by police. The three attackers were of Algerian ethnic origin and were born and educated in France and had declared this a victory in the name of ISIS.

ISIS followed up on these events with a further series of coordinated terrorist attacks that began in one of Paris' northern suburbs, Saint Denis, on the eve of November 13, 2015. Here, suicide bombers attacked the Stade de France, followed by a series of attacks in restaurants, cafés and the Bataclan Theatre. One hundred thirty people were killed with ISIS again taking responsibility. Then, on March 22, 2016 Brussells' international airport and subway system were attacked by suicide bombers with ISIS again claiming responsibility.

The world's reaction was swift and raised phobia levels toward Islam and the Muslim people to new highs and served to illustrate how phobic reaction can foment in any society, given the right combination of events and attitudes. In essence, as countries around the world were taking in new immigrants, they were also witnessing a surge of a different kind that both frightened and intimidated the status quo. With the world's continuous involvement in trying to eradicate the ideology represented by ISIS and its increasing number of jihadist recruits, a new wave of anti-Islamic and anti-immigrant sentiment has begun to spread globally. This sentiment is propelling foreign leaders into delivering strong statements declaring multiculturalism to be a failed endeavor leaving immigrants in precarious and dangerous positions across the globe. In Germany, for example, Chancellor Angela Merkel faced a new challenge when over 500 complaints were launched by females who were sexually assaulted on New Year's Eve in Cologne in 2015. The attacks involved groups of drunk and aggressive young men which witnesses and police said were of Arab or North African appearance. This led to renewed cries for Merkel's resignation and how she had handled immigration policy and multicultural initiatives.

In 2016, the debate has become further intensified with ISIS stepping up its campaign to create an Islamic state in Syria, resulting in a wave of refugees fleeing the war zone. This refugee crisis has resulted in great pressure for countries worldwide to open their doors to a new wave of immigrants. As a consequence, a renewed debate and criticism of multiculturalism and its policies has further intensified. In Canada, planes arrived with Syrian newcomers, their numbers swelling over 50,000 and representing the largest resettlement initiative since the "boat people" from Southeast Asia in the 1980s. This new wave of immigration has stirred debate around religious identity within a religiously neutral society. As Pfrimmer (2015) states "Multiculturalism has served Canada's national narrative well. But it does not consider adequately the important role faith plays for people, especially for newcomers. We all have examples where religious belief can exacerbate problems" (para. 9).

Government Response to Multiculturalism's Challenges

Ley (2010) describes the evolution and growth of Canada's multicultural policy, referring specifically to a period between 2004 and 2005, when the Annual Report on the Multiculturalism Act stated "As society has evolved and needs have changed, so too have the priorities of the Multiculturalism Program"(Government of Canada, 2006, p. 9). As discussed in the first chapter, key areas in the report emphasized active citizenship over the presentation of heritage cultures, including:

(1) Fostering cross-cultural understanding,
(2) Combating racism,
(3) Promoting civic participation, and
(4) Making Canadian institutions more reflective of Canadian diversity.

The latest data released by Statistics Canada (2011) highlight the growing linguistic, cultural, and religious diversity across the country. Unlike the previous waves of immigration, newcomers have become more visible religiously, ethnically, and linguistically, sporting characteristics that set them apart from other, previous European immigrants. Although it can be argued that the multiculturalism debate/discussion surrounds all linguistic groups, Taylor (2012) states that current rhetoric around multiculturalism in Western countries has essentially grown into a debate about Islam and Muslims. The Muslim wave of immigrants coming to Canada today not only possess physical differences, but also display religious differences not previously witnessed to such a large degree in previous waves of immigration. It comes as no surprise then that, within the Canadian context, which in many ways echoes the challenges faced across the world, one specific need articulated is for clear policies dealing with religious identities.

In an effort to provide an overview of regional trends with respect to the situation of minorities, the research arm of the Multiculturalism and Human Rights Branch at the Federal Department of Canadian Heritage commissioned a report involving six regions that recommended ideas for future research themes (Government of Canada, 2006, p. 9). While Kymlicka emphasized that the situation for minority groups was in no way similar to the condition in Europe, he did highlight areas that needed attention.

All the regional reports emphasized the importance of further research on (religious) diversity in Canada. Specific research questions were singled out by Kymlicka (2010) among the several presented. Traditionally, multiculturalism in Canada has worked with and through organizations defined, in particular, along lines of ethnicity (e.g., the Canadian Ukrainian Congress) and race (e.g., the Urban Alliance on Race Relations). Questions included:

- *How are organizations and social movements defined along lines of religion similar to, or different from, those based on ethnicity and race?*
- *How do multiculturalism programs and consultation procedures initially designed for issues of ethnicity and race need to be revised to deal with religion?*
- *Insofar as multiculturalism does adapt to address issues of religious diversity, how does this relate to principles of "secularism" that underpin contemporary liberal and democratic principles of government?*
- *Does the principle of "reasonable accommodation" provide an adequate and sufficient basis for addressing claims by religious minorities in Canada?*

All the regional reports raised concerns around the need to maintain and enhance the commitment to the struggle against racism and racial discrimination (Kymlicka, 2010). Under this heading three more specific research questions stood out among the several discussed.

(a) What is the link between racism and religious intolerance (i.e., how is anti-Muslim prejudice reinforcing and transforming older forms of racism)?
(b) What is the role of the media in dispelling or reinforcing stereotypes and what kind of strategies are appropriate for addressing hate speech?
(c) How can multiculturalism contribute to the action plan against racism?

Kymylika (2010) identifies three distinct silos (On the "silo" metaphor in relation to Canada's diversity policies, see Kymlicka (2007) within which diversity policies in Canada typically function. These silos contain separate laws, constitutional provisions, and government departments that deal with multiculturalism as it responds to ethnic diversity which arises from:

(1) Immigration,
(2) Federalism and bilingualism in response to the French fact, and
(3) Aboriginal rights for First Nations.

Kymlicka (2010) notes that these diversity policies need to be separately distinguished in that none can individually encompass a distinct historical legacy.

Ley (2010), in his succinct analysis of the current challenges the Canadian government faces vis-à-vis the official Multicultural Act, also draws attention to wider global debates around foreign policies dealing with increased tensions with the Muslim world at large. He argues, as proposed by critics of this policy, the controversy is not just about multiculturalism promoting segregation amongst minority groups living in Canada, but also about the greater international movement that rejects Western foreign policy. For example, based on a survey of one thousand British Muslims, Mirza et al. (2007) produced a report for the conservative think tank Policy Exchanges entitled *Living Apart Together*. The report indicated that British foreign policy mattered more to respondents than did economic and public services issues or even ethnospecific Muslim issues such as discrimination.

In Canada, Justin Trudeau's liberals won a majority government in 2015 and brought Canadians to a new juncture where experts articulated some hard facts about multiculturalism. These questions were framed around the issue of identity politics and were most visible when the question of the niqab (appropriateness of covering the face or not in certain situations) was brought to the forefront, striking deep at the heart of Canadian identity with references made to barbaric cultural practices, among other things. The government was called into question around who a Canadian really is, and who belongs and what that belonging looks like. The issue of the niqab struck deep at who we think we are as Canadians. At the same time, Justin Trudeau's victory speech (2015) included a pledge to restore what he called "our enviable inclusive society." However, as admirable as Trudeau's words may have sounded, the issue around phobic reaction and multicultural policy is far from resolved. Much remains to be examined, studied, and articulated.

It was shortly after the ISIS attacks in Brussels that the Canadian government announced the creation of a new office that would help respond to the radicalization threat posed in the country. The office of the Community Outreach and Counter-Radicalization Coordinator has as its mandate to provide leadership concerning the Canadian governments' response to radicalization. In addition funds will be provided to support community outreach, research, and coordination between federal-provincial and international initiatives to address the issue of radicalization. With this office the government is also initiating other "immediate measures" announced in the budget including the restoration of funds to "heavy urban search and rescue task forces" in several cities, bolstering government networks and cyber systems security, and reopening search- and -rescue station (Butler, 2016, para. 4–5). The Canadian governments' proactive stance seems to be centered on preventing radicalization. By creating policies aimed at combating and preventing radicalization, the hope is to then prevent people from joining organizations such as ISIS and therefore lessening the number of terrorist attacks. With a decreased number of terrorist attacks, government can focus on the safe integration of new immigrants into the country and lessen the fear of the other. Prime Minister Justin Trudeau's vision of a multicultural Canada has remained consistent with that of his father Pierre Trudeau's. The complicating factor that did not exist in the elder Trudeau's time is the volatile situation being witnessed worldwide that happened to coincide with a new wave of immigrants whose beliefs and culture are unique and different from previous waves of immigrants. The compounding challenge is the fact that, on the one hand there is a ready group of immigrants who want to come to Canada and start a new life here in a Canadian context, and on the other hand, the very nature of this new culture is being put under the microscope because of dangerous and threatening forces that serve to undermine Canada's original multiculturalism objectives.

In sharp contrast to Trudeau's visionary statements around multiculturalism, other parts of the world have shaped their policies in a different manner. Germany's Chancellor Angela Merkel, for example, has lamented multiculturalism: "Whoever seeks refuge with us, our laws and traditions must be respected and they must learn German. Multiculturalism leads to parallel societies and multiculturalism thus remains a living lie." This is not the first time Chancellor Merkel has lamented multiculturalism. Germany is not alone in its opinions. Other European countries have followed suit.

Across the ocean, the UK's policy makers have also shaped immigration legislation around classifications that promote categories defined by ethnic and cultural boxes. All members (of a culture) associated with a minority faith, for example, are considered to be in the same category and heterogeneity within a community is not taken into consideration, the idea being that each category represents a single voice and vision toward culture and faith. Such a tendency on the part of policy makers encourages people into identifying with particular ethnic and cultural boxes (Malik, 2015). He describes the consequence of this practice as "the creation of a more fragmented, tribal society, which has nurtured Islamism."

The strategy adopted by the French government is also noteworthy. During the 1970s and early 1980s, French authorities took a relatively laid-back stance on multiculturalism, generally tolerating cultural and religious differences at a time when few within minority communities were expressing their identity in cultural or religious terms. Then President François Mitterrand even coined the slogan "droit à la différence"— the right to be different. With approximately five million Muslims of North African origin, France is considered to have the largest Muslim population in Western Europe. With the passage of time, however, tensions with the North African community in France increased, and this policy was abandoned, and a more hard line approach adopted with an emphasis on assimilation. Immigrants trying to enter France after the Second World War experienced considerable racism and challenges in terms of successful integration into mainstream society. Yet, according to a 2011 poll conducted by l'Institut Français d'Opinion Publique (Ifop), only forty percent of North African immigrants call themselves "observant Muslims"—and only twenty-five percent attend Friday prayers. Interestingly, most of the youth that rioted in 2005 in the French banlieus did not even see themselves as Muslim. Nevertheless authorities failed to recognize the systemic racism faced by youth and instead came to label the issue as one related to Islam, hence giving voice to rising islamophobia. "Islam became symbolic of the anxieties about values and identity that now beset France" (Malik, 2015). Regardless, the contrast with the position articulated by the current Canadian Prime Minister Justin Trudeau, is stark: Malik (2015) says it well, "Countries with a strong national identity—linguistic, religious or cultural—are finding it a challenge to effectively integrate people from different backgrounds. In France, there is still a typical citizen and an atypical citizen. Canada doesn't have that dynamic. There is no core identity, no mainstream in Canada. There are shared values—openness, respect, compassion, willingness to work hard, to be there for each other, to search for equality and justice. Those qualities are what make us the first post national state." It remains to be seen whether this philosophy behind Canada's demographic holds. In addition, pluralistic democracies such as Canada rarely agree about the definition of identity. This is due in part to the multifaceted means through which one can express one's (Canadian) identity. Being Canadian means different things to different people. And it is therefore, probably more fitting to talk about Canadian cultures and identities in the plural, with continued conversation about who we are as a people. Even as recently as the 2015 prime ministerial elections, the question of identity rose up as a strong election platform and continues to be an up front and centre topic. Justin Trudeau summed it up: "You don't have to choose between the identity that your parents have and being a full citizen of Canada" (Chen, 2016).

Trudeau's words, reassuring as they are, point to the dilemma lived by newcomers. Under the umbrella of the Multicultural Act there is a sense of cultural neutrality (Simpson, James, & Mack, 2011). Canadian multicultural policy and its accompanying Act are rooted in the value systems of the represented "founding partners" of Canada. In fact, multicultural policy has not really been about maintaining one's culture within a larger neutral sphere, but rather about looking at the deeper challenges that arise when an immigrant disembarks to make a new home in a new country. These challenges include how work and school life will be portrayed, what life in general will be like, and, in short, how one's identity will be defined within society. The onus, then, is placed squarely on the immigrant to unravel his or her identity. The work, however, runs much deeper in that the immigrant must learn to successfully navigate his or her way through a country's cultural complexities. Nevertheless' within multiculturalism policy there exists a dichotomy in which, on the one hand, governments encourage cultures to preserve and embrace features of their unique identities, while, at the same time, there is pressure to conform to the ideals of "neutral universal culture." In the twenty-first century, this has been exacerbated by the war on terrorism and what is perceived to be religious ideals that are circumspect. Multiculturalism ties into gaining identity through like mindedness and the challenge, then, is how to accomplish this when there seems to be so much difference in thought, religion, life style, and attitude.

It becomes important then to frame multiculturalism in terms of understanding relationships. There are two words that come to mind that help to better understand the underlying tensions involved: Universal and Connect. Being familiar with the etymology of these two words can aid in the comprehension of how multiculturalism policy can be framed within the idea of understanding relationships. "Universal" is defined as "pertaining to the whole of something specified; occurring everywhere," from Old French *universel* "general, universal" (12c.), from Latin *universalis* "of or belonging to all," from *universus* "all together, whole, entire." "Connect" comes from the verb to connect (v.) mid-15c., from Latin *conectere* "join together," meaning "to establish a relationship" (with) (Online Etymology dictionary, 2015).

The etymologies of *universal* and *connect* clearly indicate different conceptions of how to understand relationships. Universal pertains to that which belongs to all, whereas connect speaks to the establishment of relationships. Connect refers to something that one does, and it does not follow a pre-established rendering of what the terms of that connectivity ought to be. Therefore, that which is named as universal ought not to be conflated with interconnectivity. Interconnectivity indicates establishing a relationship while drawing upon differences that are present. Universal conceptions of relationships, even in their most open manifestations, rely on a central idea to which all can relate. In fact, the way multicultural policy is framed is completely devoid of the idea of building relationships. Moreover the policy seems to exist almost in a vacuum and only provides a superficial take on identity and human relationships.

As multiculturalism continues to dominate the cultural and social makeup of so many countries in the world a central question becomes: how are societies reconstructing themselves and redefining their national identities? Tawil & Harley, 2003 ask who has the power to essentially define "official identity" and secondly how this is accomplished? These two researchers promote education and curricular reform as a means to help define national culture and identity through language policies, social studies, and using subjects such as history, geography, civics, literature, and religion as ways in which education can be the "primary and contested terrain within which the structure of national identity is formed."

The complexities of the goals and expectations of our current education system are born out of immigrant roots (albeit roots of yesteryear) and schools are experiencing similar realities as is society. This is affected equally by the world situation and the political forces at play. In fact, it could be the education system itself that helps to overcome the modern day challenges of multiculturalism. Canada has a role to play in leading the charge in better understanding the current immigrant question. When a society works to encourage its citizens to build authentic relationships, propelled by education, the result can be an understanding of how people can live together and still maintain their unique attributes. Nevertheless, multicultural policy around the world does not reflect these two concepts. In fact, it almost becomes a default logic, reflected not only in the day-to-day operations of a country, but also in its educational curricula, something experienced on a daily basis by virtually any young person attending the country's schools. The Social Studies curriculum in Alberta, Canada, for example, carries with it a focus on difference, how to react to differences and yet, its approach to difference is categorically designated. The meaning of difference, therefore, becomes lost. It is true that particular notions of difference are essential to ensure cohesion and ensure Canada's economic growth on the world stage. However, when differences exist in the interests of social and political stability, resulting in an imbalance, the prerogative of the Canadian nation-state is lost. When this occurs, it results in limiting of the interpretation of difference to government policies and legislation. To be sure, it is only those conceptions of difference that are acceptable and officially endorsed that are represented in the Canadian imagery (Donald, 2015). In essence, if immigrants and newcomers wish to partake in full and equal access to opportunities in the public sphere, they essentially have to separate their "cultural differences" from the Canadian imagery (Kallen, 2003, p. 180).

Such a vision is problematic, as the notions of identity and belongingness that define the fabric of the country cannot possibly respond to every aspect of newness or difference brought into the land. Moreover, it seems that multiculturalism defines difference as being culturally and ethnically different. This has given rise to a very limited understanding of difference and creates a sense of resentment and hostility toward all who do not represent Canadian ideals and values. This can be seen in the case of narratives around head coverings and any other manifestations of religious affiliations, as they are not perceived as representing part of the prescriptive definition of what can be viewed as the archetype of a true Canadian. As a result, there is an implicit assumption that, under the Canadian umbrella of multiculturalism, certain codes or norms are more acceptable/preferable than others.

In other words, ways of knowing and being that are not seen as in line with the predictive and fixed identity constructions of multiculturalism are regarded as a problem and a hindrance to unity. Canadian identity has long been associated with the concept of allowing cultures to breathe, to relish their sense of being and individuality and yet, the twenty-first century frames the Multiculturalism Act in a different light, discouraging the immigrant from developing his/her own identity. The very notion of multiculturalism today pressures many Canadians to believe that they need to forgo their own sensibilities in order to be privy to mainstream society's privileges. When society places impositions on how to live and survive, a troubling scenario unfolds, one that is rearing its head in Canadian, as well as other cultures worldwide.

Engaging with difference under the umbrella of multiculturalism remains a challenge. One of the major concerns with respect to this is the idea of civic engagement and relationship building among people of all ethnicities and faiths. Identity politics play a pivotal role in this discussion as they provide a window into individual perspectives and understandings of difference. While the proponents of multiculturalism espouse a universal characteristic, I suggest this does not go deep enough into the fabric of relationship building that would explore how people can truly connect.

Within a multicultural framework it is important to consider how society can engage in meaningful relationship building that is both empowering and identity affirming. When peoople begin to recognize how the terms "connect" and "universal" intersect, it may help them to create communities that are more cohesive and engage in critical dialogues that enhance unified and cohesive images of society. So, what a Muslim or a Jew or a Sikh Canadian have in common can only be determined through relationship building where we begin to share and construct a joint Canadian multicultural narrative.

Today, the debates on multiculturalism continue and, along with them, a common theme has surfaced: the need to better understand the nature of the challenge we face today. The question of belonging and identity has emerged as a very critical aspect of the debate, and while sociopolitical events may not specifically reflect the failure of multiculturalism, they point to a very serious issue that contemporary society is facing. Zakaria (2013) draws attention to the importance of building support groups that will help the younger generations to overcome any feelings of alienation, specifically making use of the example of Muslims in Europe. He argues that European countries have recognized that their indifference to new cultures is creating a culture of mutual incompatibility. As a result, one of the European initiatives has been an attempt to integrate Muslim immigrants, engaging all levels of government to include Muslims in mainstream society and also to nurture a more modern, European version of Islam. Also included in this initiative is the creation of Islamic councils, funding provisions for cultural activities, and presentation in public forums and encouraging mindfulness of religious practices and holidays.

There is no doubt that, whether in the presence or absence of multicultural policies, foreign policy has become a huge concern for Muslims living in the West. Ley (2010) reiterates:

> High levels of immigration, poverty and social exclusion have generated apartness and the leading of parallel lives. Hostile difference, currently the mobilization of small but militant Islamic cells in Western cities, derives its primary sustenance from an international movement that rejects Western foreign policy in the Middle-East. These irritants of integration policy need fuller attention, in place of the fire drawn toward the inflated target of multiculturalism (p. 204).

These trends have propelled countries such as the United Kingdom, the Netherlands, and Germany into viewing Muslims through the same lens, painted with the same brush. Sociopolitical world events such as the events of 9/11, the Boston bombings, and the like have undoubtedly perpetuated and entrenched "Muslims as chimerical others" (Allen, 2010a, p. 86). (Paris attacks, sexual assaults of women on New Year's Eve in Germany). As a result, much of the world currently identifies Muslims as either terrorists, waging war against Western culture, or apologists who defend Islam as being a peaceful religion (Sardar, 2002).

By examining how phobias emerge out of world events and what humanity can do to mitigate them, society can work toward a better solution to eradicate them, rather than relying on the notion of "letting time heal all wounds," as it has in the past. It is time to ask some pointed questions relating to how phobias and barriers toward successful integration can be removed and a positive transition can occur from being an immigrant, an alien in one's nation, to a successful, participatory member of that country and culture. Understanding the phobic reactions of society toward any cultural group requires a thorough examination of both sides' reactions.

- Is there a way to overcome some of the challenges society is facing?
- What does a social phobia do to a society?
- What are the ramifications for the culture affected by sociophobic reaction?

This chapter has explored some of the challenges facing government as regards multiculturalism. A government's primary objective as regards their immigrant population is, and continues to be, to foster meaningful civic engagement and global citizenship within this group. Worldwide, a certain societal distrust among its citizens with respect to immigrant populations has always occurred, and immigrants' lives have been punctuated with this and other challenges, including social separation and economic marginality. Canada has shared in this phenomenon and today, this seems even more apparent with one specific group of immigrants: the Muslim population. Government's challenge is to seek a way in which a religiously and culturally different immigrant group can successfully navigate its way through Canadian society.

The chapter following explores these questions and attempts to help the reader to comprehend the complexity of the current situation regarding sociophobic reaction and how society has been reacting to it. The chapter provides concrete examples and gives the reader a clear understanding of the more recent evolution of sociophobic reaction and government perspectives.

References

Allen, C. (2010a). *Islamophobia*. Farnham, SRY: Ashgate Publishing Group.

Blanshard, P. (1984). *American freedom and Catholic power*. Westport, Connecticut: Greenwood Press.

Burns, J. F. (February 5, 2011). Cameron criticizes 'multiculturalism' in Britain. *The New York Times*. Retrieved from http://www.nytimes.com/2011/02/06/world/europe/06britain.html?_r=0

Butler, D. (March 22, 2016). Budget 2016: New office aims to counter violent radicalization. *Ottawa Citizen*. Retrieved from http://calgaryherald.com/news/local-news/islamic-radicalization-of-canadian-youth-raises-alarm-bells

Carrothers, W. A. (1948). Immigration. In Wallace, W. S. (Ed.). *The encyclopedia of Canada*, 3, 239–249.

Chen, S. (January 25, 2016). Justin Trudeau perfectly articulates the value of diversity in childhood, not just in the workforce. *Quartz*. Retrieved from http://qz.com/602525/justin-trudeau-perfectly-articulates-the-value-of-diversity-in-childhood-not-just-in-the-workforce/

Donald, D. (2015). *From what does ethical relationality flow? An Indian Act in three artifacts*. University of Alberta. Edmonton, AB.

Foster, L., & Stockley, D. (1988). *Australian multiculturalism: A documentary history and critique*. Clevedon, Avon: Multilingual Matters.

Fryer, P. (2010). *Staying power: The history of Black people in Britain (get political)*. New York, NY: Pluto Press.

Fujiwara, A. (2012). *Ethnic elites and Canadian identity: Japanese, Ukrainians and Scots, 1919–1971*. Winnipeg, Canada: University of Manitoba Press.

Fulford, R. (2006). How we became a land of ghettos. Retrieved from Canada.com website: http://www.canada.com/nationalpost/news/issuesideas/story.html?id=0d7e614b-786b-4aae-9535-2c588ca13a1e

Government of Canada. (2006). Annual Report on the Operation of the Canadian Multiculturalism Act 2004–2005. http://publications.gc.ca/site/eng/283594/publication.html

Gregg, A. (March 2006). Identity crisis: A twentieth-century dream becomes a twenty-first century conundrum. *The Warlus*.

Hurewitz, J. (2005). Too tolerant of the intolerant: The Netherlands' multicultural drama. *World Security Network*. Retrieved from http://www.worldsecuritynetwork.com/Other/Hurewitz-Jeremy/Too-Tolerant-of-the-Intolerant-The-Netherlands%E2%80%99-Multicultural-Drama

Kallen, E. (2003). *Ethnicity and Human rights in Canada*. Don Mills, ON: Oxford University Press Canada.

Kymlicka, W. (2007). Ethnocultural diversity in a liberal state: Making sense of the Canadian model(s). In Banting, K. G., Courchene, T., Seidle, T. J., & Leslie, F. (Eds.). *Belonging?: Diversity, recognition and shared citizenship in Canada, 3*, 39–86.

Kymlicka, W. (2010). The rise and fall of multiculturalism? New debates on inclusion and accommodation in diverse societies. In Vertovec, S., & Wessendorf, S. (Eds.), *The multiculturalism backlash: European discourses, policies and practices* (pp. 190–206). New York, NY: Routledge.

Ley, D. (2010). Multiculturalism: A Canadian defence. In Vertovec S., & Wessendorf, S. (Eds.), *The multiculturalism backlash: European discourses, policies and practices* (pp. 190–206). New York, NY: Routledge.

Luciuk, L. Y. (2000). *Searching for place: Ukranian displaced persons, Canada and the migration of memory*. Toronto, ON: University of Toronto Press.

Malik, K. (November 15, 2015). Terrorism has come about in assimilationist France and also multicultural Britain. Why is that?.. *The Guardian*. Retrieved from http://www.theguardian.com/commentisfree/2015/nov/15/multiculturalism-assimilation-britain-france

Maraia, J. (May 2, 2011). The impact of Osama bin Laden's death on al-Qaida. *The United States Institution of Peace: Making Peace Possible*. Retrieved from http://www.usip.org/publications/the-impact-osama-bin-ladens-death-al-qaida

Mirza, M., Senthilkumaran, A., & Ja'far, Z. (Producer). (2007). Living apart together. British Muslims and the paradox of multiculturalism. Retrieved from http://www.policyexchange.org.uk/images/publications/living apart together - jan 07.pdf

Pfrimmer, D. (December 18, 2015). Refugees can move us from multiculturalism to multifaithfulness. *The record.cm*. Retrieved from Retrieved from http://www.therecord.com/opinion-story/6200466-refugees-can-move-us-from-multiculturalism-to-multifaithfulness/

Prins, B., & Saharso, S. (2009). From toleration to repression: The Dutch backlash against multiculturalism. In Vertovec, S., & Wessendorf, S. (Eds.), *The multiculturalism backlash: European discourses, policies and practices* (pp. 72–91). New York, NY: Routledge.

Rose, E. J. B., & Associates. (1969). *Colour and citizenship: A report on British race relations*. London, New York etc.: Published for the Institute of Race Relations by Oxford U.P.

Runnymede (Producer). (2000). The future of multi-ethnic Britain: The Parekh report. Retrieved from http://www.runnymedetrust.org/projects/meb/report.html

Sardar, Z. (2002). The excluded minority: British Muslim identity after 11 September. In Griffith, P., & Leonard, M. (Eds.), *Reclaiming Britishness* (pp. 51–56). London, UK: Foregin Policy Centre.

Saunders, D. (2012). *The myth of the Muslim tide: Do immigrants threaten the west?*. Toronto, Canada: Alfred A. Knopf Canada.

Scheffer, P. (January 29, 2000). Het multiculturele drama. *de Multiculturele Samenleving*. Retrieved from http://retro.nrc.nl/W2/Lab/Multicultureel/scheffer.html

Scheffer, P. (2011). *Immigrant Nations: Achieving consensus on the politics of multiculturalism*. Cambridge: Polity Press.

Simpson, J. S., James, C. E., & Mack, J. (2011). Multiculturalism, colonialism, and racialization: Conceptual starting points. *The Review of Education, Pedagogy, and Critical Studies, 33*, 285–305.

Statistics Canada (Producer). (2011). 2011 National household survey: Immigration, place of birth, citizenship, ethnic origin, visible minorities, language and religion. Retrieved from http://www.statcan.gc.ca/daily-quotidien/130508/dq130508b-eng.htm

Tawil, S., & Harley, A. (2003). Education and conflict in EFA discourse. *Norrag News, 3*, 43–47.

Taylor, C. (2012). Interculturalism or multiculturalism? *Philosophy & Social Criticism, May/June, 38*, 413–423.

Universal. (2015). In *Online Etymology dictionary*. http://www.etymonline.com/index.php?allowed_in_frame=0&search=universal&searchmode=none

Watson, J. L. (1977). Introduction: Immigration, ethnicity, and class in Britain. In Watson, J. L. (Ed.), *Between two cultures: Migrants and minorities in Britain* (pp. 1–20). Great Britain: Basil Blackwell.

Zakaria, F. (April 24, 2013). Fareed Zakaria: A better way to integrate Muslims. *Washington Post*. Retrieved from http://www.washingtonpost.com/opinions/fareed-zakaria-a-better-way-for-america-to-integrate-muslims/2013/04/24/9e1ca588-ad12-11e2-b6fd-ba6f5f26d70e_story.html

Chapter III

Islamophobia: A Twenty-First Century Example of Sociophobic Development

What Does Sociophobia Do to a Society? What are the Ramifications of the Culture Affected?

Research indicates that Muslims are one of the fastest growing groups in Europe (although this has been perceived to be unreliable because of the tendency to omit religion from census questions) (Lipka & Hackett, 2015) and there is no doubt that new immigration patterns all over the world have resulted in very rapid social change. Communities affected by this change have also been witness to high sociophobic reaction to immigrant groups (e.g., Muslims); this often accompanied by criticisms that said group is unwilling or unable to fully embrace a sense of national identity and that there is a reluctance to embrace the values of the country to which they have migrated. Among sociological distinctions, the immigrant group is often perceived as having high concentrations of members living in one particular area, with segregated schools and shops. Phobic reaction is further exacerbated when the minority group displays outwardly visible symbols of identity such as specific religious clothing or religious buildings that do not conform to "the norm" of that society. Other rhetoric (Shah, 2005) helps to inflame sentiment and examples include high profile political personalities who deliberately debase a particular societal group. (For example, Pym Fortuyn, a far right Dutch politician who led his own anti-Islam party before being assassinated and Geert Wilders, leader of the Netherlands far right Party for Freedom PVV). In addition, the media fuels phobic sentiment when people read about certain practices exercised by a social group. (For example, in the Muslim example, practices such as forced marriage, female circumcision, and honor killings). Many of these reports are written from a sense of unfamiliarity with the culture and ignore or fail to mention that these occurrences are not prevalent through all immigrant groups of that culture and are often the extreme. (For example, the perception that all Mormons are polygamists.)

The tendency toward marginalizing immigrant groups has been proven historically on several different occasions. Using the Muslim example, this group has often been ghettoized and socially excluded because of perceived higher than average unemployment rates, a tendency to live in neighborhoods that experience elevated levels of poverty, and a lack of representation in leadership positions within that society. This pattern has often been perpetuated among many immigrant groups because of having a last name that sounds different (take the case of the Jewish population during the Second World War or, currently, having a Muslim sounding name) and may result in further escalation of any sociophobic reaction within that culture. In fact, a study conducted by University of Toronto researchers published in 2016 concluded that there is a disturbing trend within North America whereby people with ethnic sounding last names have been engaging in a practice known as "resume whitening" (Keung, 2016) in which candidates delete any signs of race or ethnicity from a CV in the hopes of landing employment. The study indicates forty percent of minority applicants have "whitened" their resumes by anglicizing their names and disassociating themselves from any one cultural group.

One of the most contentious issues within any country that gets to the heart about public anxieties is how to accommodate newcomers' attitudes and behaviors while continuing to uphold national values. Since

September 11, 2001 Western tensions have shaped world news and created flash points that raise broader questions regarding immigration and integration policies. The myriad terrorist attacks that followed 9/11 have only served to exacerbate fears about Muslim minorities being a security threat, including their perceived hesitancy to integrate, and their exclusion from the public discourse. In order to address this, countries have created policy in an attempt to balance the rights of the citizen with those of the immigrant and achieving this balance has not been easy. Many of the policies drafted to date have been perceived as highly controversial and it remains a monumental challenge for law makers to attempt to take the resulting public anxieties seriously and examine their root causes, while, at the same time, protecting religious freedoms. France's ban on the burqa and other head gear that covers the face or Switzerland's referendum that banned any new construction of mosque minarets are two initiatives that have drawn public support in some arenas and criticism elsewhere, and in many cases, these initiatives are perceived as being nothing more than a blatant attack on Islam. The resultant reactions for or against these initiatives have also fueled the challenge for these immigrants to effectively integrate into mainstream society, essentially barring them from living out a normal existence.

Consequent challenges arise when trying to deal with the ramifications of welcoming a culture and people that are notably different from the cultures and people who have been part of earlier waves of immigration patterns. Because Muslims are such a highly visible community in Europe, as well as in other Western countries, and their visibility is plainly obvious, public anxiety has increased in direct proportion to the number of local communities whose sociocultural makeup has been altered through immigration.

Papademetriou (2012) concludes, however, that immigration is not the only, or most predominant, driving force that dictates how society is affected by changes in its sociocultural makeup. He highlights cultural, social, economic, and political frames as well, all of which combine to impact society and he reiterates how these are areas of contestation attributed to the changes that naturally occur when new comers enter into a society that is different from the one they are leaving.

According to Papademetriou (2012) these frames all work both interdependently and independently and reflect how society changes when it's essential make up becomes reworked. The cultural frame involves a sense of losing one's identity through the gradual disappearance of language, cultural norms, and the natural spirit of the culture. When an immigrant moves to a new country, he/she effectively creates a type of new pseudo culture; one that has never been lived before as they attempt to integrate (often with limited success) into the new culture.

Papademetriou (2012) maintains that the social frame impacts general society in terms of forfeiting the "constant" within that society. Change naturally occurs when other groups add different dimensions and cause the traditional culture to become unbalanced. Oftentimes, this is viewed as a rich, positive dimension. Canada's Multicultural Act has helped here in some ways, encouraging Canadians to embrace this new "unbalanced culture." At the same time, the societal frame can act as a wedge between the longstanding, traditional society and the new, multidimensional one created with new immigrants arriving and upsetting the balance.

An economic frame, according to Papademetriou (2012) witnesses public goods and resources needing to be redistributed and costs are incurred as a direct result of immigration and integration of immigrants. The prevailing culture is naturally affected by these forces. Countries trying to help the current wave of Syrian refugees at the start of 2016, for example, witnessed a strong backlash against accepting any form of refugee for the fear that prevailing economic conditions at the time would result in tensions around job creation for a group coming into the country when jobs were scarce.

A political frame is understood when political intervention becomes inevitable and leads to societal rifts as one political party may espouse one policy and other parties another. In Canada, particularly within Quebec, the Muslim population was targeted politically through the province's proposed "Charter of Values," introduced in 2013 by the then-governing Parti Québécois under the leadership of Pauline Marois. The charter aimed at prohibiting the public display of any religious symbols including the Sikh turban, the Jewish kappa and the Muslim hijab. Lakritz (2015) accused the Québécois government of phobic reaction stating, "What's really underlying all this is Islamophobia, whose premise is that if you're a Muslim, then you are guilty of being a jihadist, and likely an ISIS sympathizer, until proven innocent, but of course, you'll never be proven innocent" (para. 7). The Parti Québecois lost the April 2014 provincial election and yet, the media reported the majority of Quebecers had favored the proposed Charter.

Also in the Canadian context, during the 2015 Federal election, a simple comment of whether or not to permit the wearing of the niqab in citizenship ceremonies polarized the entire country. Political parties made this their number one platform and yet, the woman at the heart of the controversy only wished to uphold her rights to religious freedom in Canada. Papademetriou (2012) also proposed a fourth and final frame; a security frame, implying a sense of phobia in general society in that its newest members could contribute to social unrest, illegal activity and terrorism. As one example of many, the November 2015 coordinated Paris attacks on a concert hall, stadium, subway, and restaurant all helped to fuel sociophobic reaction around the world and renewed anxiety around immigration through a perceived crack in the general societal feeling of security in that particular city.

Papademetriou (2012) emphasizes that all of these frames work in conjunction with one other and help demystify phobic reaction in so many countries today, including Canada. His premise is based on the idea that immigration becomes a "target for something over which to exercise control in a time of great uncertainty." The 2016 US primaries were a good example of this. Historians will probably reflect years from now, citing this time in American political history as being one of prejudice, racism, and phobia and the rhetoric of some of the presidential candidates touched some sensitive points around sociophobia when comments were made comparing Islam to Nazism, for example. Canada as well used an impending election as a platform to decry the Muslim factor in the country and the impact it was having on cultural, economic, political, and social mores and European politicians have also used their influence to breed sentiments of anti-Islam.

In 2011, the Public Religion Research Institute conducted a survey in which fifty-five percent of Republicans and fourty percent of Democrats in the United States believed that any terrorist attack conducted against civilians was consistent with the belief structures of the Muslim faith (Cox, Dionne, & Galston, 2011). In addition, a Brookings survey in 2015 showed that sixty-one percent of Americans maintained negative opinions of Islam (Telhami, 2015). Canada has not been immune from this type of sentiment either. Despite having a reputation of multicultural tolerance, one 2011 poll found that fifty-six percent of Canadians believe the Western World to be in "irreconcilable conflict" with Muslim society. Of 1500 respondents, fourty percent approved of racial profiling of airline passengers that looked to be Muslim (Cader & Kassamali, 2012). In Canada much of the discussion around Muslims and Islamophobia has revolved around the unfaltering opinion toward one particular member of that culture: Muslim women. Quebec's proposed Bill 94 in 2010 is a good example of this. Under this bill, Muslim women would be denied essential government services, public employment, education, and health care. In fact, Canada's version of Islamophobia has been perceived to be much more of a sociocultural phenomenon than one linking the entire group to acts of terror. A declassified ITAC report written in 2010 maintained that "Canadian Islamists are constructing 'parallel societies' where Muslim organizations "do not advocate terrorist violence but promote an ideology at odds with core Western values" (ITAC, 2010). The report went on to say "The creation of (these) isolated communities can spawn groups that are exclusivist and potentially open to messages in which violence is advocated. At a minimum, the existence of such mini societies undermines resilience and the fostering of a cohesive Canadian nation." Canada's chief concern, therefore, is not so much about Muslims planning imminent terrorist attacks but rather the threat they pose to Canada's nation building philosophy. The report calls for greater government attention paid to how Muslims think, communicate, and organize their day to day lives. At first blush, the fears and anxiety generated over the past three decades certainly may have seemed warranted because of the actions committed by extreme factions of the Muslim Faith. As stated before, these fears were not only centered in America. In 2011, a Pew Global attitude survey found that seventy-three percent of respondents in Germany, seventy percent percent in Britain, and sixty-eight percent in France are worried about Islamic extremism (Pew Research Center, 2011, p. 32). As a result, any terrorist activity has placed the world in a precarious balance between acceptance of and opposition to a different culture and has resulted in uncertainty based on fear and an increased sociophobic reaction toward this same culture. In essence, the violent nature of these attacks has directly undermined the multicultural initiatives undertaken by many countries, precipitating an unprecedented anti-Islamic tide around the world.

What follows is by no means an exhaustive list, but is representative of events (both violent and sociological) that have occurred with the objective of transforming the fundamental functions and precepts of Western society. The list is provided as an information item and also to garner proof of what has been occurring in the world to merit such anti-Islamic sentiment and to better understand the roots of Islamophobia.

April 18, 1983: United States Embassy in Beirut, Lebanon, attacked by suicide bomber.

August 7, 1998: United States Embassy in Dar es Salaam, Tanzania, and Nairobi, Kenya, attacked using truck bombs.

September 11, 2001: Four planes hijacked by 19 al-Qaeda hijackers: two planes crash into World Trade Centre and one into the Pentagon. Nearly 3000 dead.

March 11, 2004: Madrid train bombings purportedly in response to Spain's participation in the NATO force in Afghanistan.

July 7, 2005: Multiple bombings in London Underground. Fifty-three killed by four suicide bombers. Nearly 700 injured, purportedly for the UK's participation in the NATO force in Afghanistan.

September 2005: The Province of Ontario repeals Religious Arbitration Act thereby removing any legal basis for Sharia law.

June 30, 2009: Four members of Afghani descent found dead in a car submerged in a shallow canal in Kingston, Ontario. Perceived honor killing:

May 1, 2010: Times Square car bombing attempt by Faisal Shahzad, a Pakistani American working with the Pakistani Taliban or Tehrik—i-Taliban Pakistan.

September 11, 2012: United States embassy in Benghazi, Libya, attacked by organized mob resulting in the death of American Ambassador and three others.

April 15, 2013: Boston Marathon bombings. Two brothers, Tamerlan and Dzhokhar Tsarnev, plant two bombs killing 3 and injuring183 others. One day after the bombings a Grade 8 Muslim student goes to an inner city school in Toronto. A large group of Grade 8 students surround this student and say to her, "How does it feel now that you have killed so many people in Boston? When are you planning to bomb the CN Tower?"

September 10, 2013: The Quebec Values Charter is proposed and later taken off the table after the Parti Québécois is defeated in the April 2014 provincial election). Quebec would become the only jurisdiction in North America to impose a sweeping ban on religious clothing for public employees, including at school, hospitals, and court houses (including hijabs, kippas, turbans, and larger than average crucifixes warn by religious public servants).

April 15, 2014: Boko Haram, a militant Islamic group operating out of Nigeria, abducts nearly 300 girls from a school in the northeast town of Chibokk, Nigeria.

June 9, 2014: Jihadist militant group Isis proclaims the establishment of a caliphate, or Islamic state, on the territories it controls in Iraq and Syria.

June 11, 2014: The northern Iraqi city of Tikrit is seized by ISIS.

June 18, 2014: Twenty year old Somali-Canadian from Calgary is spotted in a video burning his Canadian passport, surrounded by ISIL militants.

October 22, 2014: A shooting attack on Canadian Parliament building killing an unarmed Canadian soldier.

December 15–16, 2014: A hostage taking at a café in Sydney, Australia kills three and injures four. The shooter acted alone but was a self-styled Muslim clerk who had been rejected by both Sunni and Shia members.

January 8, 2015: A shooting attack by two Al Qaida gun men on Charlie Hebdo newspaper office in Paris.

November 13, 2015: Coordinated terrorist attacks in Paris on the night of Friday November 13 by gunmen and suicide bombers hit a concert hall, a major stadium, restaurants, and bars, almost simultaneously—and left 130 people dead and hundreds wounded (BBC News, 2015)

March 22, 2016: Attacks at Brussel's International Airport in Belgium airport and in one of its subway tunnels kill 31 and injure 270.

Based on the above events, the frequency with which they are happening, and the societal reaction that have spawned, it would appear that visible minorities (in particular Muslims), rather than making progress to becoming more accepted and integrated into the society in which they have chosen to live, have regressed in their progress since the dark days of 9/11 (Singh, 2016). Singh (2016) goes even further to suggest that using the suffix "phobia" may even seem insufficient as reaction to the most recent attacks has turned fear and mistrust toward Muslims into more than a sociophobia. The words "hatred" and "hostility" are being employed more frequently to describe current popular reaction and the most recent attacks have instigated a renewed feeling of mistrust and suspicion against Muslims.

In spite of the plethora of events that have precipitated these anti-Islamic feelings, further examples illustrate that sociophobic reaction is not only initiated from the fallout of a terrorist attack. Halstead (2015) postulates how the development of social phobias also seems to coincide with the apparent choices that a cultural community makes when organizing its way of life and the discourses and realities that propagate in the form of cultural or even religious values. A clear example of this lies within the traditional Muslim immigrant group of whom many have not readily adopted Western values (often seen as more liberal) and, in many cases, choose to adopt a value system based on a more theological foundation. In addition, they are electing, what is perceived to be by Canadian standards, to live in abidance with a lifestyle interpreted as being a rejection of Canadian (Judaeo-Christian) values, even as they move into a new and different cultural setting.

Such was the case, for example, in Canada in 2010 when Aqsa Pervaiz was murdered by her father and brothers, an honor killing that took place because she was, according to her family, seemingly manifesting behaviors that were too westernized. This tragic event developed into an excellent display of the cultural and ideological clash of the Muslim culture with mainstream, Western society, manifesting itself not only in North America, but worldwide.

In a further example, recent alleged threats to Canadian security have become often improbable figures: from Xristos Katsiroubas and Ali Medlej, ordinary-seeming high school students turned hostage-takers in Algeria, to John Nuttall and Amanda Korody, alleged drug-addicted rockers and late converts to radical Islam (Globe Editorial, 2013). In more recent analyses of acts of violence often committed by younger men who are either first- or second-generation immigrants, analysts are putting forth the notion of "self-radicalization" and examining the societal aspects that can potentially play a role in promoting feelings of alienation and marginalization among youth.

During the tragic events of the 2013 Boston bombings, for example, there was much scrutiny and talk about two brothers who were originally from Chechnya and accused of perpetrating the bombings. Media reported in great length about their interests and educational accomplishments and their integration and transition into American society and the educational setting in North America. Their friends spoke of their successful integration into North American culture and the various sports and outdoor activities in which they were engaged. Nevertheless, speculation was rife about what could have prompted two apparently well-adjusted young men to commit such a violent act. Such debates are not new and have been part of a post 9/11 culture marked by vocabulary of suspicion and anxiety. What is becoming clear, through the various testimonies being circulated through the media, is that many immigrants seem to be leading lives parallel to mainstream society and will often turn to their ethnic milieu for solace and comfort, particularly in times of distress and emotional anxiety.

Ishak and Solihin (2012) also argue that the significant role and potency of the media in the promotion of Islamophobia cannot be denied nor can its potential for the rectification of Islamophobia. Although hateful messages toward Muslims or Islam had been banned as early as the same year of the 9/11 attacks, with the field changing substantially in Web 2.0 applications, social networking and a largely unregulated and robust information highway, the media has never been more pervasive, powerful, and influential.

Nasr (2013) pointed out that people are mainly afraid of Islam because they know very little about it and the media does a very adequate job of heightening phobic reaction, especially if the perpetrators of a terrorist act, for example, are young, male Muslim immigrants, as was the case with the Boston Marathon bombings in 2013. Television anchors and respectable journalists, representatives of the citizenry in charge of propagating an unbiased opinion on national media sources, have become society's role models and have helped to shape people's opinions. Nasr (2013) argues that phobia has been rooted as much in the absence of information as in the presence of a skewed version of it. Nasr further iterates that the media, in tandem with Islamic organizations and Muslims in general, are in a position to send out as many positive messages and images about Islam as they do negative ones. More often than not, however, this does not occur.

These opinions undoubtedly affect the media's perspective, which results in misinterpretations and a perpetuation of phobic reaction (Amosa & Gorski, 2008; Burnett & AcArdle, 2011; Jackson, 2010; Moore, 2009; Najwa, 2011; Smith & Denton, 2005). In a similar manner, while cultural perceptions are being reimaged and reformed, at the same time western society is frequently exposed to media images depicting the negative stereotype of villainous, dark skinned Muslims with Middle East accents (e.g., Disney's animated Aladdin). In contrast, protagonists all seem to be fair skinned and retain American accents. A variety of song lyrics also suggest a stereotypical image of the Arab culture: "Oh I come from a land, from a faraway place, where the caravan camels roam, where they cut off your ear if they don't like your face, it's barbaric but hey, it's home" (Wingfield & Karaman, 2002).

Additionally, Muslims (and in particular Muslim men) acting in current movies and television shows (*G.I. Jane, The Rules of Engagement, Twenty Four* and the Netflix hit series *Homeland* to name a few examples) are often portrayed as being Arab and terrorist, oil sheikhs or tribesmen. Women are typically portrayed as belly dancers and harem girls or in meek, subservient roles. Jackson (2010) states "out of heterogeneous images and narratives ultimately emerges a common, normalized associating of Islam and Muslims with terrorism and/or conflict, violence, irrationality, and vengefulness" (p. 21). Although the media continuously claims to play a necessary role in reporting and informing the public, Jackson maintains that, after 9/11, associating Muslims with antagonistic measures (violence and terrorism) was made even more apparent. Even if the media does not mean for this association to be present, the resultant effect on the general populace is that they will deem it as normal for this association to take place. Jackson (2010) further elaborates that, "thematic, analytic, and critical lessons in media literacy must complement the formal curriculum about Islam to optimize the active awareness and critical reception of what is ultimately portrayed as normal to think about Muslims in the mass media" (p. 22). Therefore, the means used to portray stereotypical images of Muslims are not as important as the content of the messages being broadcasted and instilled in the minds of young students and the role of the media can also be immense in the portrayal of the real aspects of Islam, which are based on "submission" and "peace" (Jackson, 2010, p. 263).

The primary catalysts for any sociophobic reaction can often be traced to a lack of information coupled with an inaccurate and exaggerated knowledge aimed at inciting negative public opinion. The more the world is witness to irrational behavior on the part of a certain ethnic group, the more the sociophobic reaction tends to be. To combat this, educational institutions have been identified as the key places where phobic thought can be addressed in a positive manner and turned into a well-informed, receptive viewpoint. Today, most schools operate on the premise of an egalitarian agenda. To be specific, this assumption neither denounces education of the extreme Islamic stance, nor does it propagate a more even-keeled approach. Incidences of institutional neutrality such as this can result in Muslim students either being ignored, or the creation of a culture of resistance in response to the ridicule and verbal abuse these students face from other students. Institutional failure to recognize the presence of Islamophobia in society causes a long-term negative effect, and reneges on the educational contract to provide a safe and secure learning environment for all students. This results in the solidification of Islamophobia in the education system, upon which the onus for the correction of any misconceptions of Islam and Muslim culture lies solely on the Muslim students or their parents. This creates a serious imbalance between the two sides and progress toward reconciliation is compromised without an opportunity to question each other when problems arise and to listen carefully to either side. In any case, such discussions often never arise, as no safe spaces are created and any criticism from either side is perceived as a threat.

Rizga (2016) compels us to think about this in a different manner. She cites several examples in which the rhetoric of educators and other significant adults have contributed to general anti-Islamic feeling. One such example notes how many students are bullying their Muslim peers, calling them "terrorists" and other derogatory names while, at the same time, teachers and administrators often do not take proactive measures to mitigate these reactions. In spite of the negative perception toward "the other," slow, but sincere, initiatives are beginning to be undertaken in various schools across North America, aimed at trying to build understanding and communication among cultures. One such idea is proceeding in a San Francisco Bay area high school in which students have formed a Muslim Student Association in an effort to work collaboratively with teachers and Muslim youth. They meet once a week to build social awareness where students lead discussions around the complicated political issues in the Middle East as well as issues they can address at their local school. All this occurs in order to reduce the incidence of Islamophobia occurring within their classrooms. One student in particular commented on how a teacher facilitated an open discussion on the Paris attacks with Latino, Black, White, and Asian students. This enabled students to have an open dialogue with their Muslim peers to better equip them to understand what had transpired and equip them to be able to form educated opinions without deliberate hurtful reactions.

Other points covered in meetings include strategies to reduce Islamophobic language and discuss other types of racial stereotyping that include anti-Black comments and critical narratives around undocumented Latinos. As a further example, Muslim students in one school suggested another potential intervention that included a panel discussion around what is happening in the Middle East and to include Muslim authors in the library's book collection as well. These educational initiatives represent a growing initiative that includes teachers, researchers, and students across the country who are trying to uncover and implement different strategies to reduce Islamopohobia, particular within educational institutions (Rizga, 2016).

There is no doubt that the education system can play an important role in addressing Islamophobia, however as Rizga (2016) reiterates, there is no one-size-fits-all solution and to propose a curriculum change across the board could have negative repercussions. Educational initiatives such as those that have taken place in the San Francisco Bay Area, have worked there because of the cultural makeup of the student population. In another school the initiative may be entirely different. One thing is clear, however. The role of the teacher is paramount in helping students understand the ramifications of phobic comments and feelings. Sociophobic reaction and its consequences can be better understood if teachers work in tandem with students to help them understand why they are saying or feeling something and whether or not it is a rational fear or something that is a product of what is happening around them. Sleeter's (2011), research uncovered how students from ethnically diverse backgrounds thrive in an atmosphere where they are allowed to interact and discuss widespread stereotypes within the classroom. In this environment, teachers make connections between course work and the everyday realities of their students' lives, including issues such as war, racism and poverty. Such approaches have been identified as "ethnic studies curricula," helping students to understand the factors contributing toward social unrest and social phobia. Incorporating comparative studies into this allows students to understand the similarities and differences between present-day immigration patterns (such as the Syrian refugees) with those of previous waves of immigration.

Lulat (2006), charted out the parameters of Islamophobia and how it relates to the different challenges that Muslims have to face within their own communities, including the challenge of living in a Muslim minority or majority areas. Allen (2010b) demonstrates how researchers build and bolster the premise that Islamophobia as a concept has no inherent merit or basis for its continued existence. Nonetheless, the fear can be demystified by a discussion around Islamic principles and core Islamic values, without any defense coming from any opposing camps. The adequate introduction of values and notions through various approaches can successfully lead to softening and subsequent diminishing or complete removal of Islamophobia. These include such concepts as knowledge, charity and the welfare state and include culturally responsive teaching practices or specific pedagogical strategies such as 'face to faith'(Haynes, 2011). Allen (2010b) points to the importance of addressing the prevalence of phobias against Muslims, particularly within educational settings, and representing and introducing Islam in a positive light. Equally important is generating discussion about the necessity for peaceful acknowledgment of the multitude of ideas and the hegemonic dominance of certain idea sets which cause other ideas to be marginalized, thus generating biases against them, often in the form of phobias.

Ozanne (2006) and Shah (2011) summarize the reservations that communities share about Islamic values and the effect those values might have on society. Both Ozanne and Shah focus similarly on the curriculum that is taught in Islamic schools and attempt to juxtapose them with the secular curriculum that is taught in Western schools. This is done not for comparative purposes, but more to verify how they complement one another and they suggest combining Islamic and secular curricula together to be offered in schools to western students when it is appropriate to do so. Shah (2011) specifically discusses how scholars in their research have "been exposed to a variety of resources that will be useful in the classroom, including Islamic literature, poetry, 'passion plays,' calligraphic art, and the meaning of the Qur'an in support of certain Islamic beliefs" (p. 35). Ozanne (2006) argues that, if curriculum were to be enhanced by the introduction of certain modules and courses that would introduce students to Islamic values, there could result a substantial decrease in sociophobic reaction, specifically to the Muslim culture. This decrease would ultimately set a precedent about the successful use of intellectual instruments borrowed from the marginalized culture under attack to reduce the phobia regarding that very same group. Zine (2001) raises an important question: If a country finds it justified using affirmative action to rectify any institutional inequality or marginalization occurring for any social group, why cannot educational institutions do the same for students who are targets of social phobias?

Researchers all seem to agree that the education, demystification, and accurate portrayal of social groups needs to occur through greater interaction and active guidance by teachers within educational institutions. As important as educational initiatives are, however, governments and institutions alike must also examine the "new history" being made among Muslims who are living within non-Muslim cultures, not to conquer them (as with countries like Turkey), nor to be chased out of them (as in the Spanish case). The reality is Muslims are living and working within a society, coexisting peaceably within a culture that has other religions.

Religious and visible minorities have long experienced racism, hatred, and vile comments. Ultimately, feelings of phobic reaction around the world need to be replaced with dialogue and respect between and among *all* cultures. Until then, our society will be at a loss as to how to live in peaceful harmony (Alawa, 2014). Any initiative to address the current spectre of mistrust depends on a variety of answers to provocative questions:

- As globalization and economic interdependence of the world continues to expand, multiculturalism and mutual coexistence seem even more imperative. What role can education play in this development?
- Can Canadian curricular objectives include more discussion on the multicultural question, going beyond the French/English/Native perspectives and incorporating the "new immigrant," one with a different physical appearance, a different religion?
- What role can the Muslims themselves play in helping to differentiate themselves from the image of extreme religious terrorists and into a well-adjusted, participatory member of society, integrated into Canadian culture, yet still maintaining his/her own sense of identity?
- In essence, how can a new immigrant live within current multicultural policy and objectives and what role, if any, can our current education system play to help navigate toward an answer to these questions?

There is no doubt this world has seen an upswing in phobic reaction toward Muslims. Much of the reaction has been precipitated by world events which have resulted in many people associating Muslims with violence, irrationality, and a sense of vengeance. As a result, it is becoming more and more apparent that, in order to mitigate the resultant feelings of mistrust and suspiciousness, education systems and schools can come to play a major role.

These questions are explored in the next chapter as the reader is taken to a new level of understanding integrating the education system as a catalyst in helping to demystify the concept of sociophobic reaction.

References

Alawa, L. (January 21, 2014). Muslim women targeted in latest example of Islamophobia. *Policy.Mic*. Retrieved from http://mic.com/articles/79507/canada-s-muslim-women-targeted-in-latest-example-of-islamophobia

Allen, C. (2010b). An overview of key Islamophobic research. http://www.amnesty-polizei.de/d/wp-content/uploads/Muslime+Polizei.pdf

Amosa, W., & Gorski, P. C. (2008). Direction and mis-directions in multicultural education: An analysis of session offerings at the annual conference of the National Association for Multicultural Education. *Multicultural Perspectives, 10*(3), 167–174. doi:10.1080/15210960802198373

BBC News. (December 9, 2015). Paris attacks: What happened on the night. Retrieved from http://www.bbc.com/news/world-europe-34818994

Burnett, B. M., & AcArdle, F. (2011). Multiculturalism, education for sustainable development (ESD) and the shifting discursive landscape of social inclusion. *Discourse Studies in the Cultural Politics of Education, 31*(11), 43056. doi:10.1080/01596306.2011.537070

Cader, F., & Kassamali, S. (2012). Islamophobia in Canada: A premier. http://islam.ru/en/content/story/islamophobia-canada-primer.

Cox, D., Dionne, E. J., & Galston, W. (September 2, 2011). What it means to be an American: Attitudes in an increasingly diverse America ten years after 9/11. Retrieved from http://www.brookings.edu/research/reports/2011/09/06-american-attitudes

Globe Editorial. (July 7, 2013). Terror, 'self-radicalization' and the beat-cop approach. *The Globe and Mail*. Retrieved from http://www.theglobeandmail.com/globe-debate/editorials/terror-self-radicalization-and-the-beat-cop-approach/article13046572/

Halstead, J. M. (2015). Islam, homophobia and education: A reply to Michael Merry. *Journal of Moral Education, 43*(1), 37–42. doi:10.1080/03057240500049281

Haynes, C. C. (2011). Putting face to FAITH: A free education program helps students talk about religious diversity. *Educational Leadership, 69*(1), 50–54.

Ishak, M. S. B. H., & Solihin, S. M. (2012). Islam and media. *Asian Social Science, 8*(7), 263–269.

ITAC. (2010). http://www.itac.gc.ca/bt/index-en.php

Jackson, L. (2010). Images of Islam in US media and their educational implications. *Educational Studies: Journal of the American Educational Studies Association, 46*(1), 3–24. doi:10.1080/00131940903480217

Keung, N. (March 17, 2016). Jobseekers resort to 'resume whitening' to get a foot in the door, study shows. *Thestar.com*. Retrieved from https://www.thestar.com/news/

immigration/2016/03/17/jobseekers-resort-to-resum-whitening-to-get-a-foot-in-the-door-study-shows.html

Lakritz, N. (March 5, 2015). 'Je suis rania' must become the new outcry. *Times Colonist*. Retrieved from http://www.timescolonist.com/opinion/columnists/naomi-lakritz-je-suis-rania-must-become-the-new-outcry-1.1782232

Lipka, M., & Hackett, C. (April 23, 2015). Why Muslims are the world's fastest growing religious group. *PewResearchCenter*. Retrieved from http://www.pewresearch.org/fact-tank/2015/04/23/why-muslims-are-the-worlds-fastest-growing-religious-group/

Lulat, Y. G.-M. (2006). Comparative perspectives on Islamic identity and issues of education in the aftermath of September 11, 2001 (Essay Review). *Comparative Education Review, 50*(3), 518–527. doi:10.1086/505285

Moore, J. (2009). Why religious education matters: The role of Islam in multicultural education. *Multicultural Perspectives, 11*(3), 139–145. doi:10.1080/15210960903116563

Najwa, A. (2011). A place for informal learning in teaching about religion: The story of an experienced non-Muslim teacher and her learning about Islam. *Teaching and Teacher Education: An International Journal of Research Studies, 11*(3), 139–145. doi:10.1080/15210960903116563

Nasr, V. (2013). *The dispensable nation: American foreign policy in retreat*. New York, NY: Anchor Books.

Ozanne, W. I. (2006). Confronting Islamophobia in educational practice [Review of the book Confronting Islamophobia in educational practice, by B. Van Briel]. *Comparative Education Review, 42*(2), 283–285. doi:10.1080/03050060600628116

Papademetriou, D. (2012). *Rethinking national identity in the age of migration. Council statement from the 7th plenary meeting of the Transatlantic Council on Migration*. Washington, DC: Migration Policy Institute.

Pew Research Center. (2011). Muslim-Western Tensions Persist. from Pew Research Center http://www.pewglobal.org/files/2011/07/Pew-Global-Attitudes-Muslim-Western-Relations-FINAL-FOR-PRINT-July-21-2011.pdf

Rizga, K. (January 26, 2016). The chilling rise of Islamophobia in our schools. *Mother Jones*. Retrieved from http://m.motherjones.com/politics/2016/01/bullying-islamophobia-in-american-schools

Shah, A. (March 31, 2005). War, propaganda, and the media. *Global Issues: Social, Political, Economic and Environmental Issues That Affect Us*. Retrieved from http://www.globalissues.org/article/157/war-propaganda-and-the-media

Shah, N. (2011). Combatting anti-Muslim bias. http://www.tolerance.org/magazine/number-39-spring-2011/feature/combating-anti-muslim-bias

Singh, A. (2016). The new wave of Islamophobia: Being Sikh or Muslim in the age of Donald Trump. http://www.salon.com/2016/01/03/the_new_wave_of_islamophobia_being_sikh_or_muslim_in_the_age_of_donald_trump/

Sleeter, C. E. (2011). *Keepers of the American dream: A study of staff development and multicultural education* (Vol. 121). New York, NY: Routledge.

Smith, C., & Denton, M. L. (2005). *Soul searching: The religious and spiritual lives of American teenagers*. New York, NY: Oxford University Press.

Telhami, S. (December 9, 2015). What Americans really think about Muslims and Islam. Retrieved from http://www.brookings.edu/blogs/markaz/posts/2015/12/09-what-americans-think-of-muslims-and-islam-telhami

Wingfield, M., & Karaman, B. (2002). Arab stereotypes and American educators. In Lee, E., Menkart, D., & Ozakawa-Re, M. (Eds.), *Beyond heroes and holidays: A practical guide to K–12 antiracist, multicultural education and staff development* (pp. 132–136). Washington, DC: Teaching for Change.

Zine, J. (2001). Muslim youth in Canadian schools: Education and the politics of religious identity. *Anthropology & Education Quarterly, 32*(4), 399–423.

Chapter IV

Toward Culturally Sustaining Pedagogy and Antiphobic Initiatives

Carl Abou Samah is a young Canadian hip-hop artist and songwriter who uses the name Karl Wolf. Interesting to note, in the midst of an age characterized by increasing mistrust between Western and Middle Eastern cultures, Wolf has achieved prominence and built a following among both North American and Arabic youth and has become an ambassador for Arabic culture in North America.

"Centuries of mistrust between cultures won't be overcome with a song or two. However, a new generation on both sides is listening to an artist whose music and personal history represents a fusion of two worlds. Sometimes, one experience in common is enough to start a conversation between strangers that can lead to understanding and friendship."

(Kielburger & Kielburger, 2013, para. 13)

On June 21, 2014 a rally was held in Calgary to protest the terror group Islamic state of Iraq and the Levant (ISIL, also known as ISIS). Robertson (2014) quotes Kablan, a national security director of the Conference Board of Canada indicating "rallies such as this event might help prevent others from taking up ISIL's cause. There are Canadians from different backgrounds willing to stand up and say terrorism and violence is wrong."

"Parents can only give good advice or put their children on the right paths; but the final forming of a person's character lies in their own hands." – Anne Frank

"The problem with Islam today is misinterpretation, and extremism. The solution is a leader." – Jari Qudrat, director external affairs for the World Religions Conference, York University

Educational initiatives exist in Canada that are designed to create an awareness of what Islam is all about, engaging students at all levels in conversations around Islam and the Muslim culture. As an example, educational institutions across Canada have begun holding what is commonly being called, Muslim Awareness Weeks. This initiative has also garnered input from the Muslim community itself around sociophobic attitudes that are being perpetuated towards and within their culture. This is an extremely important move on the part of the Muslim culture in North America. As long as the Muslim community remains silent to any world events and their repercussions, it will remain on the shoulders of Western society to dispel any phobic reaction. This is a heavy responsibility, especially in the face of what has been currently occurring around the world.

Multiculturalism policy and the role of education implicitly operate on the premise that in the absence of either, society tends toward the formation of preconceived notions or opinions that will place a certain minority or cultural group at a social disadvantage.

There is no doubt that many cultures, from the Judaic Faith worldwide, to the Roma community in continental Europe, and more recently, the Muslim community in the Western hemisphere, have experienced phobic reactions from society at large. In all three examples, the author suggests the implementation of a multicultural education initiative and the resultant systematic undoing of prejudices ultimately have led or can help lead to the subsiding and even disappearance of such phobias.

Several models have been suggested as a possible means to helping squelch sociophobic reaction in any specific culture. Ladson-Billings (1995) suggests a "next step" in theoretical pedagogical practice as including a model that hinges on student achievement, but also adds the dimension of helping students to accept and affirm their cultural roots and identity. Her curricular suggestion would include the development of critical perspectives that aid in ending the perpetuation of inequities that schools (as well as other institutions) have helped to perpetuate. Ladson-Billings calls this pedagogy "culturally relevant pedagogy" (p. 469). Traditionally, culturally relevant pedagogy (CRP) has helped form the basis of other pedagogies attempting to create cultural empowerment within a society.

Ladson-Billings's (1995) landmark article entitled "Toward a Theory of Culturally Relevant Pedagogy" has become ubiquitous in educational research circles and in teacher education programs. Her work to this end issued one of the most important theoretical statements regarding CRP and her premises have laid the foundation for how students of different cultures can maintain their heritage culture while at the same time being encouraged and empowered to critique the dominant power structures. Although Ladson-Billings' work primarily highlighted the success of teachers of African-American students in particular, her work resonates with other cultural groups as well. Teachers and university-based researchers have been inspired by what it means to make teaching and learning relevant to the languages, literacies, and cultural practices of students and their communities.

Ladson-Billings' formulation clearly laid the ground work for helping to perpetuate the heritage culture of students of color and encouraged students to critique dominant power structures. As the twenty-first century is rolled out, however, and new population dynamics have occurred worldwide, it has become apparent that much of the work completed under the umbrella of culturally relevant pedagogy has come up short of Ladson-Billing's goals. Research now indicates that even the term *relevance* itself has deficiencies by its very definition. As evidenced by Gutiérrez and Rogoff's (2003) work, it is quite possible to be relevant to something without that something being ensured of its continuing presence in students' repertoires of practice within classrooms and communities. New research indicates culturally relevant pedagogy and, specifically, the way it has been employed in teacher education and practice, should be revised forward from the crucial work that has been completed to this point. Gutiérrez and Rogoff (2003) proposed a cultural historical approach that focused researchers' and educators attention on how the "histories of engagement in cultural practices" vary according to the group. In other words, rather than focusing on specific traits within a certain culture, what became the overarching emphasis was the history of people and their specific cultural activities coupled with their experience, Their use of the word "regularities" helped to define how cultural communities can be understood through common ground rather than focusing on their differences.

Paris' (2012) helped advance this idea even further with the notion of "culturally sustaining pedagogy" (CSP), an initiative that sought to embrace linguistic, literate, and cultural pluralism within the school system. While Ladson-Billings' (1995) raised important questions about culturally relevant pedagogy and introduced ways and models for redirecting thinking and doing for better learning outcomes, it has only been recently that the question of sustainability has been tackled. With CSP, linguistic, literate, and cultural pluralism work in sync as part of the democratic process of schooling and as a needed response to demographic and social change. CSP, then, uses education as a link that desires to focus on sustaining pluralism and overcoming the challenges of social justice and change in ways that previous iterations of asset pedagogies did not. Paris (2012) indicates that up to this point in history, most educational goals have revolved around policies and practices aimed at developing a monocultural and monolingual society. Paris suggests research and practice need to resist that impulse toward a one culture, one language type of society and begin to embrace cultural pluralism and cultural equity (p. 93). Paris' (Paris, 2012) platform maintains school pedagogy requires more than young people being exposed to responsive or relevant cultural experiences; sustaining the cultural and linguistic competence of communities must work in tandem with competence in the culture and linguistic makeup of the dominant culture. The explicit goal of CSP, then, is to support multilingualism and multiculturalism in practice and perspective for students and teachers and to seek to "perpetuate and foster—to sustain—linguistic, literate, and cultural pluralism as part of the democratic project of schooling" (Paris, 2012, p. 95).

In addition to its goal of combating current educational and social policies, CSP also offers a further rationale as part of honoring and valuing communities of color. Educational goals have too long relied upon languages, literacies, and cultural ways of being as a means of accomplishing this. Although research and theory have demonstrated there is inherent value in fostering a pluralist society through education, CSP highlights a wholly instrumental, contemporary rationale. Given North America's current demographic shifts toward a majority multilingual, multicultural society of color (Gracia & Cuellar, 2006; Smelser, Wilson, & Mitchell, 2001; Wang, 2013), embedded in an ever more globalized world, it is no longer viable to think of simply allotting value to all communities; what counts now more than ever are the skills, knowledge, and ways of being needed to succeed both in the present and into the future. The assimilationist and antidemocratic/monocultural educational policies that have long held power across North America in particular, are no longer viable and need to be augmented and reviewed in light of CSP and what it can offer to the new demographic shifts of the Western world.

Within the US education system, deficit approaches to teaching and learning have been echoed for decades. The deficit approach operates under the assumption that language, literacies, and the cultural ways of being of many students and communities of color are deficiencies that need to be overcome if the dominant language, literacy, and cultural ways of being demanded in schools are to be learned. However, collaborative work between researchers and teachers eventually proved deficit approaches to be untenable and unjust (Cazden & Leggett, 1976; Heath, 1983; Labov, 1972; Moll, 1992; Smitherman, 1977). As societal demographics continue to shift, so does the "culture of power" (Delpit, 1988). Increasingly, that culture can no longer be assumed to be that of the White, middle-class linguistic, literate, and cultural skills and ways of being that were considered the sole gate keepers to the opportunity structure in the past.

As an example of this, court rulings and subsequent policies throughout the 1960s and 1970s required American schools to attend to the different languages represented within their system (e.g., Spanish, Navajo, Chinese, African American Language) and, to a lesser degree, the cultures of communities of color. New pedagogies began to emerge that repositioned the linguistic, literate, and cultural practices of working class communities (i.e., impoverished communities of color) as possessing great resources and assets that could honor, explore and extend, rather than diminish the potential they had within society. As a result, throughout the 1990s and into the twenty-first century, using this research as a foundation, *asset pedagogies* were enacted and understood in ever more complex ways by educators and researchers (Ball, 1995; Garcia, 1993; Ladson-Billings, 1994; Lee, 1995; MaCarty & Zepeda, 1995; Moll & González, 1994; Nieto, 1992; Valdés, 1996). CSP, then, has become increasingly relevant, not only to promote equality across racial and ethnic communities, but also to ensure access and opportunity.

Another strategy discussed within the last few years is a theory known as culturally responsive teaching (CRT). As the term suggests, CRT is a model of pedagogy and educational curriculum that uses the cultural characteristics, experiences, and perspectives of ethnically diverse students as conduits for teaching them more effectively. The assumption is that learning is made easier and more thorough when students' lived experiences and frames of reference are shared in common with their academic knowledge and skills. This creates a more meaningful, high interest learning experience and helps educators become more responsive to various cultural needs and increases their sensitivity to culturally and religiously diverse students. Gay (2000) and Fitchett, Starker, and Salyers (2012) discuss the example of a Social Studies course in which the use of a culturally responsive teaching model was made during preservice training.

This type of classroom is becoming more and more prevalent in Canada as a rising number of non-Caucasian students enter classrooms in the wake of new waves of migration patterns and growth in the demographics of already resident populations. Traditionally, Social Studies courses have been deemed to be Eurocentric and thus create a challenge for the integration of culturally responsive teaching into the core of the course (Fitchett et al., 2012, p. 586). Fitchett et al. state that CRT is currently widely advocated and advances beyond the intuitive idea of simply being good teachers to becoming socio-politically conscious educators with a willingness and motivation to work with diverse groups of students. Fitchett et al. (2012) discuss the CRT model provided in the work of Gay (2000, 2002) who lays out five basic principles of the CRT approach. These are "(a) developing a cultural diversity knowledge base, (b) developing a culturally relevant curriculum, (c) demonstrating cultural caring and building a learning community, (d) exhibiting effective cross-cultural communications, and (e) delivering cultural congruity in classroom instruction" (p. 588). The application of CRT in the schools discussed by Fitchett et al. (2012) successfully resulted in a positive attitude shift toward teaching in diverse classrooms, demonstrated by educators manifesting increased confidence therein.

Nevertheless, Moje and Hinchman (2004) chose to challenge CRT in favor of yet another paradigm. They stated, "we prefer to simply talk about *responsive teaching*" (p. 322). "By responsive teaching, we mean that which merges the needs and interests of youth as persons as well as learners of new concepts, practices and skills." This thereby coins a new term known as culturally responsive learning (CRL), whereby the responsibility for cultural awareness and best practice is shared amongst the teacher, the student and the school in general.

It is important to note that approaches such as CSP, CRT, and CRL have not gone unnoticed on a global level. Countries across the world have begun to actively pursue initiatives to mitigate the effects of sociophobic reaction toward minorities, and, in particular, the Muslim population. The analysis of various research initiatives as indicated below, conducted in international arenas, demonstrates the importance of systemic intervention at all levels. Although not an exhaustive list, it is apparent that these initiatives share the common goal of introducing sustainable mechanisms that work.

Following are some examples of these initiatives:

Table 4.1. International Initiatives to Reduce Islamophobia.

Initiative	Description	Impact
Steven Lawrence Inquiry Report (Macpherson, 1999)	Steven Lawrence: A black British man murdered in a racist attack. Case became a cause celebre one of the highest profile racial killings in UK history. Purpose of the inquiry: To identify lessons learned from the investigation and any racially motivated crimes.	Profound cultural changes to attitudes toward racism and the police as well as toward the law and police practice.
Report by the **Commission on British Muslims and Islamophobia** (Stone, 2004)	Model of good practice for all British communities outlining four different kinds of interaction to foster a better understanding: Pragmatic contact, e.g., in relation to regeneration and neighborhood renewal. Political contact, e.g., with regard to Israel/Palestine. Theological contact, (e.g., regarding similarities and differences between the two religions). Ethnic cultural contact (e.g., looking at shared and ethnic cultural practices).	According to Stone (2004) no substantial steps have been taken to work in this direction.
The importance of teaching Islam in East Asia at the University level. (Wai-Yip, 2008)	Curriculum to help students understand that they are the potential peace makers within a future global multiethnic and multiglobal society. Introducing students to counter sociophobias and misconceptions about the religion by: Nurturing students' sensitivity to the historical legacy of civilizational coexistence. Promotes students' conflict resolution abilities. Broaden students world map and teach cultural geography. Incorporate the teaching of Islam to counter the hegemonic narrative of islamophobia.	Seems to be present only as lip service due to historical and political factors and China's sheer size and global position.

Initiative	Description	Impact
Northern Thai research about local historical legacies of three minority communities. (Wallace & Athamesara, 2004)	Case study involving teachers and interviewing people of various ages to uncover and identify any cultural inconsistencies in the collective narrative. Not related to the Islamic context but clarifies the possibility of a tailored curriculum sprouting out of the efforts of a local population.	Documented process in the form of a curriculum for future students to experience culturally responsive learning.
Germany initiative to introduce primary school lessons in Islam using state-trained teachers.	Working with Muslim students to better integrate them and counter growing influence of radical religious thinking. The Hesse curriculum effectively places Islamic instruction on equal footing with similarly state-approved ethics training in the Protestant and Catholic faiths. Offers young Muslims a basic introduction to Islam as early as first grade.	Increased focus on education and greater inclusion for Germany's approximately four million Muslim.
Facing History and Ourselves: Nonprofit international educational and professional development organization.	https://www.facinghistory.org/ Engaging students of diverse backgrounds in an examination of racism, prejudice, and antisemitism in order to promote the development of a more humane and informed citizenry. Staff members work in ten locations across the United States and Canada.	Significantly increases engagement, critical thinking skills, empathy and civic responsibility among young people.

Initiative	Description	Impact
(Re)embracing diversity in New York City public schools: **Educational outreach for Muslim sensitivity**	http://www.mei.columbia.edu/research.shtml Initiation of a special curriculum, *(Re)embracing Diversity in New York City* aimed toward the wellbeing of New York City's school children.	Supports educators in how to foster tolerance and diversity to nurture post 9/11 healing process.
Face to faith Free program for twenty-first century secondary schools.	https://www.facetofaithonline.org/ Launched by Tony Blair Faith Foundation Encourages dialogue on faiths, cultures, and beliefs while teaching about the role they play in addressing the most pressing global issues of our time. Uses a monitored on line community with thematic teaching modules and free video conferencing to link schools around the globe.	Has created an awareness in students around: environmental issues, wealth and poverty, global health issues and personal expression using the latest technology.
California three Rs **Rights, responsibility, and respect**	http://ca3rsproject.org/ A Project of the California County Superintendents Educational Services Association and The First Amendment Center. A document outlining the rights, responsibility, and respect needed for citizens to maintain civil discourse when engaged in disagreements because of deeply held beliefs.	Broader dissemination of resources and helping to create an awareness of the Islamic faith.

Initiative	Description	Impact
Faces of Islam: Stories and quotes from a diverse group of everyday Australian Muslims.	http://facesofislam.com.au/ The community has been put under the spotlight in a new project aimed at dispelling misconceptions about Islam and its followers.	Has demystified Muslim people by breaking down false stereotypes, and sharing common experiences, to bring people together.
Tanenbaum Centre for Interreligious Study	https://tanenbaum.org/programs/education/curricula_for_educators/ Encourages classroom discussion around multiculturalism through activities embedded into the core curricula (literacy, math, science, etc.) Key values include respect for difference, curiosity and open mindedness in an effort to help students navigate the way through their world.	Faith-driven peace activists from around the world reduce violence and build cultures that reject extremism.

In recent days, the term "globalization" has been at the forefront of conversations that revolve around building not only nations, but collective identities. At the same time, with all the movement occurring in the world's demographics, there is also an emphasis on building strong communities within one's immediate surroundings. In other words, there is a diminished emphasis being placed on the "homeland," and more cultural formation centered on the here and now. Taking an example from the Sikh community in British Columbia, Canada, one can see a focus being placed on building roots that are no longer influenced by an exterior, far away source in India. Rather, British Columbia Sikhs are concentrating on building a cohesive community within the province that has its own unique characteristics.

In a similar vein, the various subgroups within the Canadian Muslim community are also developing a type of increasingly hybrid identity within a Western, Canadian context. This new identity focuses on sustainable forms of grouping that, hopefully, will provide future generations with safety and security and a sense of belonging to the culture into which they have been born that melds into the Canadian identity. In other words, they are not seeking to be, for example, Iraqi or an Iranian in Canada. Nor is their quest so much faith-based as it is being aware of their faith within the context of their immediate space and it is this space, the local community in which they now live that is being redefined.

The multicultural society that Pierre Elliott Trudeau had envisioned in the twentieth century is being redefined. As we think about mosques, for example, we see Muslim immigrants, and now, second-generation Muslim Canadians grouping around these spaces. To be sure, there is a tendency, as has occurred in previous immigration patterns, for all these people to stick together within the confines of their own cultural community. In reality, however, more and more they see their world closed within the walls of their particular community, generating not a separate cultural grouping per se, but, rather, what is being witnessed is almost a type of reclusiveness, almost a backlash against the multiculturalism envisioned by Trudeau. Instead of communities living together in tolerance and understanding, intermingling with each other and circumventing the barriers of faith and culture, there seems to be a trend allowing cultures to develop their own definition of "home." Instead of "home" being the "old country" of the post-Second World War society, "home" has developed into a sense of rising consciousness that the world has changed and the religious and cultural practices undertaken in the "old country" are being redefined and reworked in a different country. People are very aware that religious and cultural practices have evolved as the next generation begins developing a life that is not based on eventually moving back "home." As people new to a country become very aware they are on the margins and there is a clear consciousness of the difference between them and other members of the population, identity politics have taken on a new role. Herein lies the danger of this consciousness: it almost helps communities to segregate themselves even further from one another, a push-pull mechanism that comes with the liberties and affordances of multicultural discourse. This mentality almost assists communities to stay away from each other. The new immigrant is very aware of his/her right, for example to practice religious observances and dress the way he/she wishes but at the same time their sense of identity becomes a question with which they need to grapple as they grow and mature into another generation.

In spite of all the rhetoric around immigration, phobic reaction and how new immigrants self-identify, it remains important to acknowledge that global citizenship still remains a common goal of all curricula, whether in Canada, Australia, the United Kingdom, or Europe. At the same time, however, society continues to maintain a phobic discourse, reminding us that the barriers and walls are not getting any lower and communication is still a challenge because of this phobic discourse. Today, foreign policy, ideologies of war, and groups like ISIS exerting worldwide influence all contribute to making the necessity for a new type of curriculum; a curriculum that helps to address how new immigrants to a country can embrace their culture, while at the same time affording them the opportunity to be counted as one of the many cultural components that help define who we are as a global entity, wherever we may live.

The charter of rights and freedoms attempted to ensure there would be no barriers to self-recognition. However, the minute one considers this from the perspective of public spaces, then public interaction in communities and models of learning in society are brought into the public arena. Judgment is passed as to the compatibility of these models of thinking, living or even learning with current policy. Donald Trump, in his bid for the US presidency, for example, has been so successful/popular because he has fed into the notion that this divide is insurmountable and that the only way to overcome this rising fear of "the other," in this case the Muslims, is to ban them or get rid of them, not allowing them to enter mainstream society. The same can be said for the prevailing sentiment in Western Europe. From an educational perspective, it is an interesting phenomenon, representing a return to former conservative values. However, society needs to be open to new people to see how we can all live under harmonious values and systems, even though differences exist. Policy has become a platform to stop this kind of movement, threatening the stabilization of society. In effect, society needs to acknowledge that different cultures are already represented in all walks of life, their identities extending beyond just their professional designations into the whole spectre of the way they live and intermingle with their coworkers, peers, and families. It is ironic that, as small as our world is today, with people traversing cultures and countries in a constant pattern of travel, we still remain so close-minded to the reality of cultures living together in harmony within one country. This seems to occur because when people are put into situations where they see the landscape shifting so dramatically, as it is today, they find the social conditions to be threatening. Often, this occurs as a result of a lack of mutual dialogue around what to do to improve these social conditions and an examination into how identity can actually be brought into a public space where there can be some discussion around phobic reaction.

There remains, therefore, an urgency within the context of education to have that kind of discussion within schools and to investigate innovative curricula that can assist teachers and students in overcoming these misunderstandings. The simple concept of the cycle of life demonstrates how these new generations are feeding into the system and comprise the future. We need to help this new generation rise to the challenge of living together in a peaceful world. Current curricula do not live up to this challenge.

Current Curricular Limitations

Alberta's current Social Studies Program of Studies reflects Canadian multiculturalism through all grade levels. It helps to perpetuate this notion and focuses principally on the history of the First Nations and Canada's evolution as a bilingual and officially multicultural country. The concept of difference is valued and endorsed within the program of studies and the nation's "pluralism" builds upon Canada's historical and constitutional foundations, which reflect the country's Aboriginal heritage, bilingual nature and multicultural realities (Alberta Eudcation, 2015, p. 1). The curriculum outlines and emphasizes the need to educate and inform youth on how to respect differences and regard them as strengths for the benefit of the nation (pp. 1–5). Not only does the Program of Studies recognize the pluralistic nature of society, it also acknowledges the crucial link between identity and citizenship and their intimate ties to aspects such as culture, language, environment, gender, ideology, religion, spirituality, and philosophy (p. 1). The curriculum attends to the idea of difference, but with a focus primarily on the First Nations, Inuit and Metis cultures, official bilingualism, immigration, and multiculturalism. Essentially, the concept of difference is framed as being beneficial to the Canadian culture, society, and economy and is manifested as a celebratory form of multiculturalism. The assertion is that Canada as a society attends to the notion of difference as a utility for Canada.

Although these objectives are noble in and of themselves, what is essentially lacking in the depictions and portrayal of difference is the inclusion of the more recent historical trajectory, including the arrival of immigrants from countries such as Japan, India, Pakistan, and Syria. While certain historical accounts of the immigrant experience are included (e.g., the Irish, the Ukrainians, or the Polish) rarely does the reader see discussion of how more recent immigrants (post-1980) to Canada are creating a new narrative around the questions "What constitutes being a Canadian really? and "What represents his/her life story?" This leaves something of a gap between past examples and examination of current immigration trends. The concept of difference within the curriculum is hence managed within the interests of the social and political stability of Canada. In short, Alberta's Social Studies curriculum highlights discussion around certain types of cultures and historical accounts are provided with respect to the differences manifested within these cultures. However, at the same time, other cultures do not hold a prominent position in the Canadian landscape and the curriculum does little to acknowledge the evolution of that difference in the form of newer history being created by Canada's current and unique influx of immigrants. This is a problem and a challenge that needs to be addressed.

While there are a large number of resources that address racism, sexism, homophobia, and anti-Semitism, educational resources that address Islamophobia in meaningful ways are not nearly as prolific. This is primarily due to the fact that there is a dearth of material in the Program of Studies that accurately reflects the definite demographic changes occurring within Canada. In the Alberta K–9 Social Studies Curriculum (Alberta Education, 2015), for example, the idea of diversity is explicitly discussed as being beneficial for students and all learners alike. It is difficult to create an egalitarian environment when all the necessary points of cultural diversity have not been included. If there are any resources put in to address this issue, the majority of them are described as add-ons to the current curriculum. This prevents students from being able to think critically about the world situation, and does little to encourage the development of a deeper understanding of the current social realities that surround them. In addition, it does not take into account the emerging realities in the country, particularly with respect to the Islamic culture.

Lack of information often leads to lack of understanding, which in turn leads to lack of interaction, which reverts back to lack of information. It is a vicious cycle that cannot be broken unless specific strategies are developed to enhance student knowledge and awareness. Educative processes are the natural point of intervention from which information and understanding can emerge. It is clear through academic literature that educators also feel the need to redesign and reimplement curriculum to combat a wide range of social issues and address the new reality.

The work required should be centered at the heart of a country's educational programming and demands deliberate and thoughtful curricular orientations that would hopefully promote a shift in thinking. The Stephen Lawrence Inquiry (Macpherson, 1999) attempted to apply this shift, placing an emphasis on the need to focus on issues of similarity and sameness. The report also highlighted the importance of recognizing that countries, cultures, and communities are not cut off from each other and highlighted the imperative need to bring questions of diversity, including discussions on contrasting stories and ways of doing things, to the forefront.

Zine (2004) also points out that the mere fear and distrust of Islam and Muslims does not capture the complex dimensions of Islamophobia that are embedded in society. While the case for a curricular initiative makes sense, if undertaken in isolation, such as Islamic Awareness weeks, it typically does not achieve the goal of producing counter narratives that would help the new generation better understand questions of identity and mutual coexistence. In mapping some epistemological foundations for an anti-Islamophobic education curriculum, she identifies a number of aspects that need to be confronted in the education setting. These include:

(1) "Reclaiming the stage" that would involve presenting counter narratives that enable students to critically analyze and confront sociopolitical realities.
(2) Interrogating the systemic mechanisms through which Islamophobia is reinforced, by analytically unraveling the dynamics of power in society that sustain social inequality. "Reclaiming the stage" that would involve presenting counter narratives that enable students to critically analyze and confront sociopolitical realities.
(3) Working to eliminate negative perceptions and demystifying stereotypes. As an example, Zine (2004), in collaboration with Muir (2003) developed a program call "Toward Understanding: Moving beyond racisms and Islamophobia." This program is part of the Muslim Educational Network, Training and Outreach Service and was funded by the Canadian heritage Multicultural program. The project comprises multimedia resource kits, including posters, videos, and lesson plans for interactive activities that would help students understand and challenge racism and Islamophobia. The activities compiled aim at producing counter narratives that could potentially contribute to a more positive image of who Muslims are and eliminate some of the stereotypes encountered in popular media.

Minorities are always vulnerable to being stereotyped within main stream society, and this stereotyping is present in its most hyper form amongst youth circles and social interactions. Jackson (2010) iterates the importance of first addressing stereotypical behaviors in order to rectify any misaligned thought before the formulation of any policy measures aimed at altering a school-based curriculum directed at educating youth in multiculturalism. If a curriculum is to be introduced into educational institutions to counter stereotypes and work to dispel social phobias, it has to incorporate counter measures to bring the mindset of young students toward an unbiased way of thinking on the opinion spectrum

(Jackson, 2010). With the presence of immigrants who possess a different perspective on life and society, effective countermeasures can also ensure that a democratic society, such as the United States or Canada, has the ability to act in an egalitarian manner, autonomously and informed.

If the presence of phobias in educational settings is to be countered it needs to be done through pedagogical innovation and the presence of informed and motivated teachers (Ministry of Education, 2009). Jackson (2010) notes that in many instances the pedagogical training that educators receive is often lacking and, coupled with an incomplete and biased curriculum, the message imparted often becomes sidetracked by stereotypical assumptions and marginalized ways of thinking. It is very apparent that it is a challenge trying to serve the needs of both immigrant/minority students as well as the "Canadian" student because, often, teachers themselves lack the skills necessary to successfully integrate all the various cultures in their classroom (Ministry of Education, 2009). Teachers' Federations and provincial unions have expressed concerns about this, but continuous innovation, research, and development might ultimately help create a framework and action plan, which would address the needs of the Islamic student as well as their Canadian counterparts.

The introduction of CRT courses in preservice training has resulted in teachers being better equipped to counter phobias as they occurred in classrooms and scholarly works have demonstrated that CRT is a pragmatic and successful way of achieving that. Fitchett et al. (2012) echo the view of Mitchell (2009) who advocates regular professional development opportunities for teachers including a focus on themes such as culturally responsive teaching practices and the development of multicultural awareness. According to Mitchell, the pragmatic approach to accomplish this would be to organize workshops that would target, among other things, the origin of social phobias and stereotypes and how teachers can play an active role subsiding phobias in the classroom by not making any forced value judgments.

Research indicates that children can exhibit racist attitudes as early as preschool (Aboud & Fenwick, 1999). In fact, even toddlers can form negative prejudices in an environment with "clear ethnic friction" (Cameron, Alvarez, Ruble, & Fuligni, 2001, p. 124). These writers refer to the Bar-Tal study, where Israeli children as young as two-and-a-half years old rated a photograph of a person more negatively when the person was identified as "Arab." Researchers say, therefore, that Kindergarten is an appropriate time to begin teaching civic involvement, social emotional skills, and the religions of the world, for both developmental and academic reasons. Even in environments where ethnic friction is not as pervasive, children undergo two important social cognitive transitions that can affect their development of prejudice in the early elementary grades. The first transition involves the attainment of racial constancy, when children begin to understand that "they are a member of a racial group that is unchanging over time and across superficial transformations" (Cameron et al., 2001, p. 124). This transition, occurring around the age of five, impacts behaviors and preferences in children including the way in which they view themselves and others and how they might seek information about their identity. The second transition occurs between the ages of seven and nine, when "children show a qualitatively different understanding of person traits, shifting from primarily physical and concrete, to internal and psychological" (Cameron et al., 2001, p. 124). This is also a time when children are beginning to examine "dispositional characteristics with long-lasting implications (i.e., abilities) rather than simple outcome comparisons" (Cameron et al., 2001, p. 124). It is during these two transitions that children acquire critical skills and attitudes about racial, ethnic, and religious differences. They are learning about their own identity, establishing their views of others, and embarking on a journey of asking questions about culture, race, ethnicity, religion, and identity. These transitions are key elements in the development of prejudices, because they relate to how a child learns to assign value and judgment to themselves and others. As such, during these early elementary stages of a child's development, it becomes especially important to address issues around multiculturalism and interreligious understanding.

The early elementary grades are also a critical time for learning about race, ethnicity, religion, and culture, because these concepts interplay directly with the academic content focused on families and communities that children are studying in these grades. Just as knowledge of religion is necessary for older students to understand international conflict and great literature, it is equally important for young children to learn about religion in the context of foundational concepts such as self, community, and culture.

This chapter has described the evolution of culturally responsive teaching and emerging understandings of developing sustainable models of pedagogy that respond to the changing global cultural landscape. Several curricular initiatives were highlighted to inform the reader about what is currently in place and also to create awareness around curricular limitations within already developed initiatives. The chapter ends with a call to develop antiphobic initiatives that better respond to the geopolitical shifts occurring today in parts of the world.

The critical common thread running through all these initiatives is the theme of developing a broader framework for fighting phobic attitudes against Islam and Muslims worldwide. The chapter that follows highlights features of a specific curriculum that attempts to engage educators and young learners in critical discussions about recognizing diversity, appreciating cultural contributions and achieving a basic knowledge about cultural groups.

References

Aboud, F. E., & Fenwick, V. (1999). Exploring and evaluating school-based intervention to reduce prejudice. *Journal of Social Issues, 55,* 767–785. doi:10.1111/0022-4537.00146

Alberta Eudcation. (2015). Social studies: Program of studies. http://www.education.alberta.ca/teachers/program/socialstudies/programs/

Ball, A. (1995). Text design patterns in the writing of urban African American students: Teaching to the cultural strengths of students in multicultural settings. *Urban Education, 30*(3), 253–289.

Cameron, J. A., Alvarez, J. M., Ruble, D. M., & Fuligni, A. J. (2001). Children's lay theories about ingroups and outgroups: Reconceptualizing research on prejudice. *Personality and Social Psychology Review, 5*(2), 118–128.

Cazden, C., & Leggett, E. (1976). *Culturally responsive education: A discussion of LAU remedies II.* Paper presented at the U.S. Department of Health, Education, and Welfare, Washington, DC.

Delpit, L. (1988). The silenced dialogue: Power and pedagogy in educating other people's children. *Harvard Educational Review, 58*(3), 280–290.

Fitchett, P. G., Starker, T. V., & Salyers, B. (2012). Examining culturally responsive teaching self-efficacy in a preservice social studies education course. *Urban Education, 47*(3), 585–611. doi:10.1177/0042085912436568

Garcia, E. (1993). Language, culture, and education. Review of Research in Education. *Review of Research in Education, 19*(1), 51–98.

Gay, C. (2000). *Culturally responsive teaching: Theory, research, and practice.* New York, NY: Multicultural Education Series.

Gay, C. (2002). Preparing for culturally responsive teaching. *Journal of Teacher Education, 53*(2), 106–116.

Gracia, E., & Cuellar, D. (2006). Who are these linguistically and culturally diverse students?. *Teachers College Record, 108*(11), 220–246.

Gutiérrez, K., & Rogoff, B. (2003). Cultural ways of learning. *Educational Researcher, 35*(5), 19–25.

Heath, S. B. (1983). *Ways with words: Language, life, and work in communities and classrooms.* Cambridge Cambridgeshire; New York: Cambridge University Press.

Jackson, L. (2010). Images of Islam in US media and their educational implications. *Educational Studies: Journal of the American Educational Studies Association, 46*(1), 3–24. doi:10.1080/00131940903480217

Kielburger, C., & Kielburger, M. (July 1, 2013). Karl Wolf is a bridge between east and west. *Huff Post Impact Canada.* Retrieved from http://www.huffingtonpost.ca/craig-and-marc-kielburger/karl-wolf-me-to-we_b_3187689.html

Labov, W. (1972). *Language in the inner city; studies in the Black English vernacular.* Philadelphia, University of Pennsylvania Press.

Ladson-Billings, G. (1994). *The dreamkeepers: Successful teachers of African American children.* San Francisco: Jossey-Bass.

Ladson-Billings, G. (1995). Toward a theory of culturally relevant pedagogy. *American Educational Research Journal, 32*, 465–491.

Lee, C. D. (1995). A culturally based cognitive apprenticeship: Teaching African American high school students skills in literary interpretation. *Reading Research Quarterly, 30*(4), 608–630.

MaCarty, T. L., & Zepeda, O. (1995). Indigenous language education and literacy: Introduction to the theme issue. *Bilingual Research Journal, 19*(1), 1–4.

Macpherson, W. (1999). The Stephen Lawrence inquiry. https://www.gov.uk/government/uploads/system/uploads/attachment_data/file/277111/4262.pd

Ministry of Education. (2009). Realizing the promise of diversity: Ontario's equity and inclusive education strategy. http://www.etfo.ca/AboutETFO/ProvincialOffice/EquityandWomensServices/Documents/EWS Annual Report 2012.pdf

Mitchell, L. A. (2009). *Becoming culturally responsive teachers in today's diverse classroom.* Paper presented at the 2009 American Educational Research Association Annual Meeting, San Diego, CA.

Moje, E. B., & Hinchman, K. (2004). Culturally responsive practices for youth literacy learning. In Jetton, T. L., & Dole, J. A. (Eds.), *Adolescent literacy research and practice* (pp. 321–350). New York, NY: Guilford Press.

Moll, L. (1992). Literacy research in community and classrooms: A sociocultural approach. In Beach, R., Green, J., Kamil, M., & Shanahan, T. (Eds.), *Multidisciplinary perspectives in literacy research* (pp. 211–244). Urbana, IL: National Conference on Research in English and National Council of Teachers of English.

Moll, L., & González, N. (1994). Lesson from research with language minority children. *Journal of Reading Behaviour, 26*(4), 23–41.

Muir, S. (2003). Helping children feel safe in uncertain times. http://www.etfo.ca/Resources/ForParents/IncludingEveryChild/Documents/Helping_Children_Stay_Safe.pdf

Nieto, S. (1992). *Affirming diversity: The sociopolitical context of multicultural education.* New York, NY: Longman.

Paris, D. (2012). Culturally sustaining pedagogy: A needed change in stance, terminology and practice. *Educational Researcher, 41*(3), 93–97.

Robertson, D. (June 20, 2014). Calgary Muslims stand together in protest of violent extremism. *Calgary Herald.* Retrieved from http://www.calgaryherald.com/news/Calgary+Muslims+stand+together+protest+violent+extremism/9963317/story.html

Smelser, N., Wilson, J., & Mitchell, F. (Eds.). (2001). *American becoming: Racial trends and their consequences.* Washington, DC: National Academies Press.

Smitherman, G. (1977). Talkin and testifyin. In Smitherman, G. (Ed.), *Black English and the education of Black children and youth.* Detroit, MI: Wayne State University.

Stone, R. (2004). *Islamophobia issues, challenges and action: A report by the commission on British Muslims and Islamophobia.* Sterling, BA: Trentham Books.

Valdés, G. (1996). *Con respeto: Bridging the distances between culturally diverse families and schools.* New York, NY: Teachers College Press.

Wai-Yip, H. (2008). Teaching Islam to educate multiethnic and multicultural litercacy: Seeking alternative discourse and global pedagogies in the Chinese context. *Asian Ethnicity, 9*(2). 77-95. doi:10.1080/14631360802041893

Wallace, M., & Athamesara, R. (2004). The Thai community curriculum as a model for multicultural education. *International Education Journal, 5*(1), 50–64.

Wang, H. L. (June 13, 2013). Census shows continued change in America's racial makeup. *National Public Radio.* Retrieved from http://www.npr.org/blogs/codeswitch/2013/06/13/191266414/census-shows-continued-change-in-americas-racial-makeup

Zine, J. (2004). Anti-Islamophobia education as transformative pedagogy: Reflections from the educational frontlines. *American Journal of Islamic Social Sciences, Special Issue: Orientalism, Neo-Orientalism and Islamophobia, 21*(3), 110–120.

Chapter V

Foundations for an Anti-Islamophobic Curriculum

The following three vignettes highlight fictional accounts of what the author sees could potentially occur when a teacher incorporates an anti-Islamophobic curriculum into facets of his/her classroom:

Vignette #1:
In UK Birmingham, Mrs. Wilson, a teacher in a high school Social Studies classroom is actively implementing the Education Pack "Show Racism the Red Card (2015)." This resource does not include teaching about the Islamic faith as its primary goal, but rather challenges young people to dispel the many stereotypes and phobias regarding Muslims. Mrs. Wilson has been an educator for fifteen years and has faced a variety of teaching challenges. During the past few years, however, she has become aware of a different type of issue: Increasing hostility specifically targeted toward Muslim students. Her use of this resource involves the viewing of a DVD and post viewing discussion and activities that help young people to recognize and deal with their feelings toward the Muslim culture. Mrs. Wilson uses this education pack during the module addressing racism and spends, on average, two classes working on selective topics from the resource. Students are highly engaged and have the

opportunity to critically participate in debates about discrimination, prejudice, stereotyping, and sociophobic reaction.

Vignette #2:
Mr. Murray is a Grade 7 Social Studies teacher in a Los Angeles public school. As part of the course, he is teaching his students about the various immigrant groups that have settled in the United States. Today they are learning about American Muslims. In order to explore this topic, he is using a graph resource entitled "U.S. Muslims and the Larger U.S. Population," extracted from Teaching Tolerance: A Project of the Southern Poverty Law Centre (n.d.). Together, the class works toward understanding and analyzing graphs representing the age, sex, income and education of Muslim Americans compared with the larger US population. Using this information, students are given the opportunity to clarify questions and data to provide them with a better understanding of population demographics in the United States. At its culmination, students are asked to brainstorm how this activity furthered their understanding of American Muslims in the United States. This resource helps Mr. Murray to improve his practice and to contribute to building strong community within his school, a school that welcomes diversity while giving all students the opportunity to learn.

Vignette #3:
Ms. Blanchette teaches Grade 4 in a suburban Montreal elementary school, comprised mostly of white, Christian middle class students. She recently attended a professional development session that encouraged incorporating diverse literature into literacy programs. In the list provided, she chose the book The Garden of Imaan (Zia, 2013), a story about an American Muslim girl named Aliya. As a preliminary activity, students were encouraged to write down their thoughts and ideas about Muslims. Responses included comments about praying to Allah, living in the Middle East, not speaking English and being responsible for current, on-going violence in the world. Ms. Blanchette asked her students where their opinions came from and, in response, many of them said they had seen things on television or heard their parents talking about it.

After completing the reading of the book, Ms. Blanchette launched into a conversation around what the students learned about creating opinions on their own and not stereotyping someone because of their religion or the color of their skin.

This chapter brings together the cumulative goals of this book and highlights features of one curricular initiative born out of the Canadian Islamic Congress' desire to provide a conciliatory piece of work that has as its foundation mutual respect and peace.

As the previous chapters have outlined, different cultures and immigrant groups within Canada have historically been targets of racism, prejudice, and sociophobic reaction, including Aboriginals, Asians, African Americans, and others, all of whose culture and religion contrasted with that of the White Anglo-Saxon Christian majority. Today, as much as we would like to think of ourselves as a more "enlightened" culture, significant events occurring post-9/11, and most recently during the past decade, involving individuals and groups of mostly Muslim origin, have resulted in a distinctive pattern of misunderstanding and misinformation, stereotyping and assumptions targeting these specific people. Dubbed Islamophobia, this phenomenon is increasingly impacting people's lives and is also unique in terms of its burgeoning global impact.

Using educational curriculum as a means to help young people make sense out of their world has been part of the education system for many years. This book is suggesting that, with knowledge and explanation, educators can create meaningful learning environments in which young people may create their understanding of culture from a well-informed point of view. One of the most effective ways to accomplish this is through early education and, specifically, integrated curriculum development.

Early in their respective constitutional histories, both Canada and the United States installed a policy of separation of Church and State, although Canada's policy is not as firmly entrenched as is that of the United States (Wallace, 2014). This legislation was put into effect to protect life in the New World from the kinds of religious conflict that had plagued Europe since the Reformation of the sixteenth century, and thus also ensuring those conflicts did not spill over into the political realm. Although logical and valid in theory, the policy resulted in religion and religious practice being reduced to a purely private and personal affair, thus increasing the level of ignorance about religion in the public realm. Today, religion seems to inevitably enter the public realm by sheer virtue of someone who professes following and/or believing in it while working, playing and generally living in a community. Because of this, it is important for people to understand each other's beliefs in order to help prevent any interpretation of that belief structure being based on ignorance. Smith (2008) stated that "ignorance is a source of fear, and fear is a primary source of violence." One of the most important requirements for "living together" today, in Canada, must be "learning together." This calls forth a profound ethical, philosophical and pedagogical challenge from all of us, which can be framed as Smith's (2008) simple question: "How shall we *live together*, knowing that *we are always already together*?" Taking the realities of today's classrooms into account, a twofold process is proposed:

(a) An addendum to the current Social Studies curriculum that provides strategies and concrete resources to enables educators to better understand and implement strategies to mitigate sociophobic reaction and;

(b) The provision of a practical, easy to use teachers' guide. In Canada, Zine (2004) underlines "the urgency to frame a critical pedagogical response to address and challenge the rampant Islamophobia affecting the realities of Muslims from all walks of life and social conditions." The following sections outline how this can become possible.

A New Curricular Viewpoint

Throughout Alberta's K–12 Social Studies Program of Studies (Alberta Education, 2015) students learn about their country's origins, Canada's role in significant world events, and the ways in which her cultural mosaic has shaped our society. After examining the various Social Studies curricula ranging from Grade 1–9, a diagram was created with the goal of engaging the reader in understanding key components involved in broadening the approach to the teaching of Social Studies. The visual representation below demonstrates how students can engage with diversity, specifically in the context of immigration. The figure contains four key components that should assist educators in working toward a better understanding of cultural integration in education and society.

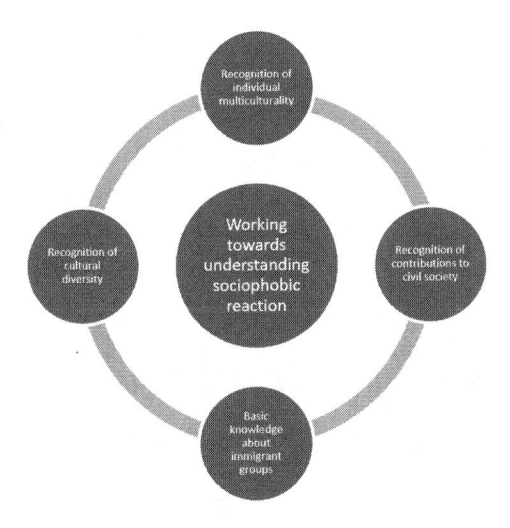

Figure 5.1. Understanding Sociophobic Reaction

Each of the four facets integrates continuously with the others in the loop, thereby creating a continuous cycle, able to commence simultaneously from any one point. All four facets; *recognition of cultural diversity, individual multiculturality, contributions to civil society,* and *basic knowledge*, are effective countermeasures to offset the scarcity of multicultural information that exists in current (Social Studies) curricula. Specifically with reference to Islamophobia, this figure highlights a model of awareness and appreciation of cultural difference. It is crucial to understand that integration and multiculturality are not singularities that will come about through a series of recommendations and outlines. Rather, it is concepts such as those represented in Figure 5.1 that must be acted upon within the classroom. The integration of this figure in a Social Studies curriculum allows for greater cultural appreciation and can go far in trying to prevent many of the assumptions and misunderstandings often prevalent in today's schools and society. This would involve encouraging critical questioning, the introduction of texts that express alternative or marginalized points of view, as well as the demonstration and promotion of active social justice. When young people are encouraged to analyze their surroundings and the content in which they are being instructed, they begin to form their own opinions. Incorporating these types of texts will encourage schools to break down barriers, bridge differences and begin to balance power relations between the dominant and subordinate cultures. With the proposed curriculum, one of the primary objectives is for young people to develop a basic knowledge about immigrant cultures, allowing them to question and acquire knowledge about these groups as it applies toward recognition of cultural diversity.

The point here is that this curriculum incorporates a foundation that can be built on what already exists in the system. Each component works with the others to shape and construct different critical repertoires in the classroom and they all have outcomes visible in practice and motivation. Integrating a more critical standpoint, with more opportunities for question making and answering, will result in classrooms that are open-minded and instructive in culture relations, as opposed to classrooms that perpetuate practices that have been in place since the era of Colonialism.

In the case of this particular curriculum initiative, young students are led simply and gently into basic knowledge and information. The purpose is not conversionary but friendly, and represents an opportunity for non-Muslim young people to better understand and gain insight into the cultural practices and identity of their Muslim friends and neighbors. Including Muslim characters and traditions into the curriculum in an integrative way gives students the opportunity to learn about Muslim practices and to be sensitive toward issues that affect Muslims in a context which does not single them out. In some sense, being Muslim is normalized.

Implementing the curriculum "Living Together: Muslims in a Changing World"

In this section we examine some entry points in the Alberta Social Studies curriculum (Alberta Education, 2015) that can be utilized as crucial steps to building greater awareness around Canada's recent Muslim immigrants and help create an awareness of the assumptions that naturally occur when one encounters difference.

Some conditions where such a curriculum would fit very well into a Social Studies classroom include the following:

- A classroom in which a student (or several students) are Muslim
- A school in which one of the primary goals is to build community, both in individual classrooms and within the school
- A school that includes an evident ELL component, where students would benefit from experiencing a connection between their first language and English

The purpose of incorporating these entry points in this book is to facilitate an understanding of how the curriculum may be used. Each entry point represents an overview of the curriculum's thematic progression and is provided to assist teachers with visualizing how this curriculum can fit into the already existing program of study.

Entry Point #1: Symbols and Celebrations

Entry point #1 focuses specifically on the diverse nature of symbols and celebrations experienced by students in that particular culture. Inquiry demands student thought and input. This can take the role of various questioning techniques based within students' prior knowledge and natural sense of curiosity. Knowing Wondering Learning (KWL) activities are very effective in this context and could be used, for example, when discussing the symbols of the crescent and the star.

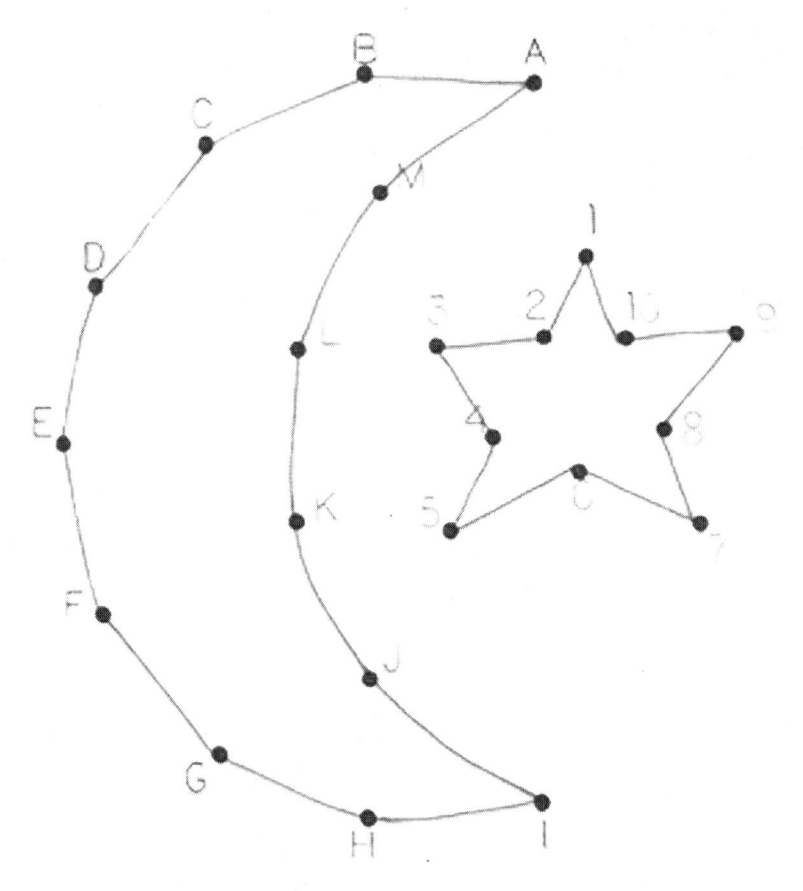

Figure 5.2. Crescent Moon and Stars

The teacher can ask his/her students, "What are symbols and where and why are they used?" Parallels can be drawn to symbols in day to day life, for example, fast food restaurant symbols, supermarket symbols, etc. The crescent and star can be compared to the Maple Leaf on the Canadian flag. Similarly, asking questions about the difference between a crescent moon and a full moon, or why farmers call a full moon a harvest moon, can lead to a discussion on Ramadan and the practices associated with it.

Using familiar activities practiced in other contexts (i.e., connect the dots, coloring) can also help students identify and remember symbols. Bringing the familiar into context with the unfamiliar helps students to better remember what has been discussed. Another example is using the concept of going on a challenging journey (e.g., a pilgrimage) to help explain the concept of Hajj. Writing can also be used as a familiar activity to draw attention to sound-symbol writing systems across the world (e.g., Arabic is read from right to left. Japanese is read top to bottom).

Class discussions can include a focus on questions such as; Who is a Muslim? What is Islam?—Muslims practice Islam and Islam is a religion. The questions can be further developed using a KWL chart of what your students think they know, what they wonder, and what they learned. Teachers may select a book of interest such as Golden Domes and Silver Lanterns: A Muslim Book of Colors by Hena Khan. This book has colorful illustrations and simple introductions to key concepts and vocabulary.

Entry Point #2: Traditions

Participating in the learning of cultural traditions allows students to become immersed in a learning experience that gives them the opportunity to "feel" the culture in a real way. The curriculum allows for a hands-on type of learning experience and also provides time for discussion and opinions on how the students felt and their reactions to studying different traditions. Discussions and activity can revolve around marriage traditions, clothing, different ways of wearing clothing (e.g., head coverings) and how clothing is contingent on different types of climates. Questions could include how we choose what to wear on our heads and when we cover our heads. A conversation around the concept of family and nuclear vs extended family can be introduced here as well, helping students to comprehend who lives in a nuclear family and who lives with extended family to appreciate various living traditions.

Many of the activities in this section revolve around literacy acquisition. Children will often use visualization before they begin to read and write. Using illustrations that represent different traditions can help them to create their own interpretation of knowledge. This can lead to a writing passage that incorporates questions such as why someone is doing what they are doing, what it would look like or feel like or smell like, and what kinds of things they may hear. In an elementary Grade 3 context, for example, this could encourage students to critically engage with an illustration while developing their writing skills and using their prior knowledge. Similarly, an activity that lends itself to discussion around writing would include a survey on other languages spoken in the classroom, highlighting the rich linguistic diversity that may be present in that particular classroom.

Entry Point #3: The Culture of Food and its Connection to Geography

Food binds people together in a natural way and a simultaneous study of Geography provides an applied method of learning about something that is always interesting. Students are made aware of the fact that Islam began in the Middle East, a geographical entity characterized by deserts, a nomadic lifestyle, and a hot climate. Because of this, the choices of diet are limited to certain foods that can grow in this type of terrain. Students are also brought into an understanding that, today, many of the foods that are eaten in North American had their origins in the Middle East. The simple reminder that many of the foods they eat in their home are also eaten by Muslims provides a sense of commonality.

To help students learn about this topic, comparative studies are incorporated to let them see and experience the differences and similarities between the two cultures. Students are also encouraged to try different recipes to further their knowledge and experience with the different types of foods.

Entry Point #4: Cultural Contributions (the Arts, the Sciences, and Civil Society)

A culture's contributions to the arts, sciences and civil society display recognition of its place in the world and its history. Learning about these gives a student a 360 degree perspective that is living and dynamic and encourages them to explore areas of study outside their own familiar territory. The curriculum outlines these well by giving ample opportunity for discussion and demonstrates the various facets of a culture and society such as those discussed below:

(a) The arts
Students learn about Islamic architecture through a study of the design of a Mosque (which can lead to a discussion around their religious significance), tombs, palaces, and forts. Tasks revolve around comparing photos of different architectural styles and discussions about their significance toward history and religion. The geographic locations of different Islamic architecture (e.g., the Alhambra in southern Spain) also help students to realize these buildings do not just appear in the Middle East but are also present in their neighborhoods in North America.

Lessons also include activities based on the study of writing systems, significant clothing (e.g., examples of headdresses, their styles and significance), and furnishings for houses (e.g., carpets and rugs). The topic of perfumes is also brought up in relation to its historical importance (e.g., frankincense was a major trading item within Christian Europe).

(b) The sciences
The sciences are used to help students understand the legacy the Muslims left throughout the early world including Botany (their ability to cultivate useful crops in even the driest conditions) and plant classification (which helped western scientists develop pharmaceutical herbs). Students are given the opportunity to do research on these various topics which allows them to better understand the uses that many common plants have in their lives today.

Mathematics is demonstrated through learning that it was the Muslims who laid the foundation for what today is modern Mathematics. Students are made aware of this through a variety of questioning activities, Math problems and discussions on the evolution of Math to the present day.

(c) Civil society
Through a series of problem solving tasks, students are exposed to how people develop social systems, order and civility in their society and this leads to quality discussion around diverse forms of decision making. Students also engage in activities that help them to understand historical events that have contributed to the Muslim faith spreading around the world. They use graphic organizers (charts and linear graphs) to compare ideas from the past with those of the present.

This helps students to understand the phenomena of trends; studying how ideas lead to trends through various media consumption and also assists students in acquainting themselves with various types of governments (e.g., comparing and contrasting the societal and governmental structures of Afghanistan, Iran, Turkey, Saudi Arabia, and Indonesia). Students are encouraged to compare and contrast authoritarian decision making with representative decision making.

Entry Point #5: Immigration

A study of immigration trends is an important facet of understanding current demographic changes within Canadian society. To develop this understanding, students examine a series of charts in order to appreciate the various different groups that have contributed to immigration patterns in Canada and, aided by statistical analysis, they also learn how to interpret data while examining how people choose where they will live when they immigrate to a new country. This section of the curriculum also exposes students to other religious groups in Canada, helping them to realize the significance and importance of the mosaic that represents our rich and varied cultural heritage.

Through watching television shows like *Little Mosque on the Prairie* and reading authentic documents about real Muslims living and working in Canada, students gain insight and come to a better understanding about the why and the how of immigration. Stereotypes are also examined through the role of the Media and personal viewpoints.

Entry Point #6: Identity and Connections

Understanding identity forms a critical facet of a child's education and of the work done in helping children become responsible and receptive individuals, open to change and flexible in their thinking. This theme is crucial to students understanding how phobias can interrupt a person's acceptance of another culture and introduces students to different choices that families make with regard to education, lifestyles, religion, and the like. Family behavior is examined through the lens of commonalities and differences between individuals. By using a Venn diagram, students can appreciate that their culture often overlaps another culture and also the realization that there are many commonalities between the two. Students are also made aware of the fact that each individual has multiple identities influenced by immigration, language, culture, education, friendships, peer pressure, religion and simply living in that country from day to day.

In fact, the whole curriculum is wrapped around the concept of identity and how it is embedded in virtually everything we do and experience. When we understand our identity, we understand ourselves and, hence, become more aware of the other.

Living Together: Muslims in a Changing World

Although this curriculum focuses on the Muslim culture, it is important to take into account that the overriding objective is to give a classroom the opportunity to learn how to appreciate diversity. This curriculum was written with the assumption that teachers, as well as students, need reference points to better understand each other. In other words, engaging with various themes puts forth the idea that we are not a singular, uniform, homogenous culture. In fact, culture is composed of many intriguing facets that, when examined more closely, permit us to gain a much needed full perspective. Initiatives such as this curriculum set the stage for what Luke (2005) explains can facilitate an understanding through "mindful exchange" between dominant and subordinate cultures. Luke suggests that the classroom can then explore the possibilities of "amalgamation" instead of "assimilation." The curriculum achieves this by pinpointing specific characteristics of an identifiable culture that open the door to discussion, empathy and appreciation of, in this case, Muslims and Islam in the twenty-first century. It is important to note that the information provided in the series is not meant to make students an expert on Islam nor the Islamic religion, but rather provide some basic knowledge about this community so constantly under public scrutiny. All this can occur in the hopes that sociophobic reaction against Canada's latest wave of immigrants can be tempered through education and awareness.

The curriculum Living Together: Muslims in a Changing World (Naqvi, 2008) is designed to supplement the learning of students in grades one to nine. It builds upon concepts already covered in the current curriculum, while at the same time incorporating aspects of Muslim culture into the classroom learning. The idea behind this integrative curriculum is to build awareness of other cultures at a young age, promote multicultural attitudes, and encourage curiosity in children about cultures other than their own. The curriculum presents opportunities for students to learn about topics they would already be learning, with the added element of incorporated examples and viewpoints from a Muslim perspective.

Below are excerpts that demonstrate how the Islamic curriculum is integrated into already developed Social Studies curricular objectives. For example, the following values statements, taken from the Kindergarten/Grade 1 Program of Studies indicate a close relationship with the proposed curriculum:

- value the diversity, respect the dignity and support the equality of all human beings
- demonstrate social compassion, fairness, and justice
- appreciate and respect how multiple perspectives, including Aboriginal and Francophone, shape Canada's political, socioeconomic, linguistic and cultural realities
- honor and value the traditions, concepts and symbols that are the expression of Canadian identity
- thrive in their evolving identity with a legitimate sense of belonging to their communities, Canada and the world (Alberta Education, 2015)

In preparation for the presentation of this curriculum units were taken from the Grade 1–Grade 4 curriculum. It is important to note that each unit is followed by a Curricular Connections section in which teachers can implement various activities that are holistically connected to the standardized curricula with which they interact on any given day. The examples below were highlighted because they accurately depict how the curriculum puts the objectives of this book into place.

*NOTE: The entire curriculum, including the teacher's guide and all student worksheets, can be downloaded through the website at: www.living-together.ca

Grade 1: Symbols and Celebrations

1. Introduction

Suggested discussion questions/activities:

(i) Have you ever seen a mosque? Where?
(ii) What makes it the same as other buildings? What makes it different?
(iii) Prior to assigning the tile picture, show the students pictures of decorated tiles. Pictures are available in *Islam* (Wilkinson, 2002, pp. 17–19).

Islam began in Saudi Arabia
Suggested discussion questions/activities:

(i) Can anyone find Saudi Arabia on the map?
(ii) What do you think the weather is like there?
(iii) What do you think Saudi Arabia looks like?

Symbols
Suggested strategy: Discuss with the students what symbols are as well where and why they are used. A good way to introduce symbols is to draw the big M on the board and ask the students what it stands for—McDonald's. Then ask if they know any others. Some examples could be the following: √ ☺ @

Arabic Writing
Suggested discussion questions/activities:

(i) What other languages have different kinds of writing?
(ii) Does anyone know a different kind of writing?

Your students may be interested in knowing that many Muslim children in Canada learn Arabic after school and sometimes on the weekends.

2. Ramadan

NOTE: Every day from dawn to dusk during the holy month of Ramadan, Muslims fast; they must abstain from eating, drinking, smoking and sexual contact and, even more than at other times, they must also avoid undesirable or imperfect behaviors.

Ramadan is the ninth month of the twelve-month Islamic calendar which is based on a lunar year.

Each lunar year is shorter by about eleven days than the solar year.

Ramadan in 2007 starts on or about September 13 and lasts for twenty-nine or thirty days. In 2008 it starts about eleven days earlier, i.e., September 3, and so on.

Suggested discussion questions/activities:

(i) What is the difference between a crescent moon and a full moon?
(ii) Why do farmers call a full moon a harvest moon?
(iii) What does lunar mean?

The Lunar Cycle

As shown in this diagram, the colored portion is what we see of the moon from earth. The new moon is not visible from earth. Ramadan begins at the sighting of the crescent moon after the new moon.

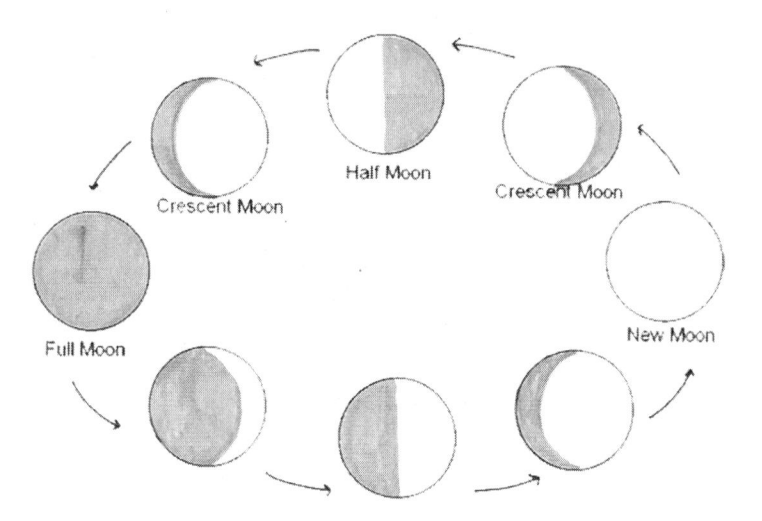

Figure 5.3. Moon Cycle

(a) The Charity Jar—Strategies

Discuss how people can help those who are needy. Ask the students if they know of a charity to which they would like to donate.

Research: Students can research to which charity they would like to give the money they collect.

How to Make the Charity Jar

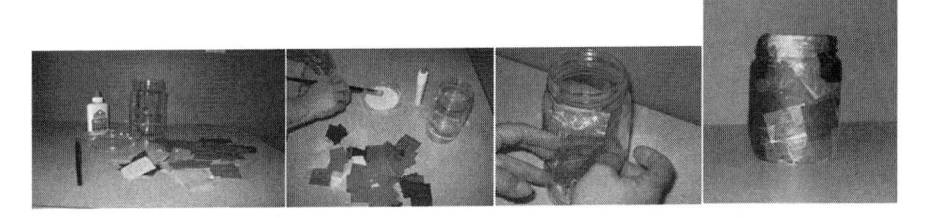

Figure 5.4. Charity Jar

These photos follow the instructions in the student book (Global Living Global Learning, 2015).

(c) The Lantern

NOTE: In Ramadan, Muslims break their fast at sunset with their families and afterward children in many Muslim countries go outdoors with their lanterns to celebrate the nights of Ramadan. In old days, lanterns had candles to give light and today most of them use battery operated lamps.

Also, huge lanterns are used to decorate shopping centers, hotels, community centers, etc. during the month of Ramadan.

Suggested discussion questions/activities:
- (i) Why were lamps used in the old days?
- (ii) What purpose do the lamps serve now?

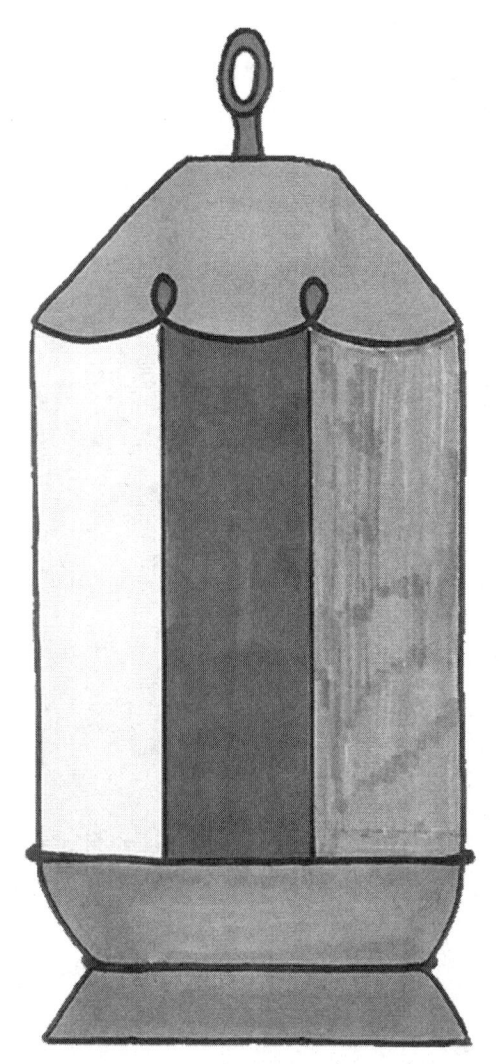

Figure 5.5. Colored Lamp

3. Eid-ul-Fitr

Class Discussion: Eid-ul-fitr

This is a celebration at the end of Ramadan. Muslims attend mosque and wear their best clothing. It is a holiday, and in Arabic, Eid-ul-Fitr means "feast."

Activity: Comparative Venn diagram

Curricular Connections: Grade 1 and 2 Social Studies

Compare and contrast festivals from your own tradition/culture.

NOTE: Eid-ul-Fitr is the first day of the tenth month of the Islamic lunar calendar.

In 2007 Eid-ul-Fitr was on or about October 13 and in 2008 was about eleven days earlier, i.e., October 3.

Eid-ul-Fitr is a day which marks the end of Ramadan, the month of fasting. Eid means feast or celebration and Fitr means "to break the fast." On that day a Muslim wakes up very early and then after praying the morning prayer, eats a small quantity of food (usually few dates) and a glass of water, symbolizing he/she is no longer fasting. Everyone, including children, put on their best new clothes.

Muslims then attend special congregational Eid prayers held in mosques or in large open areas (weather permitting), stadiums or arenas. They chant together, pray together, and the Imam offers a short sermon (khutba). Worshipers greet and embrace each other after the congregational prayer then they visit family and friends in the same city or in other cities and enjoy eating special Eid cookies and sweets.

(a) Review assignment with the students prior to them doing it themselves.

For students who do not observe festivals or other celebrations, they can talk about a special day they remember when something wonderful happened.

4. Hajj

NOTE: The journey to Makkah (Mecca) is obligatory once in a lifetime for every adult Muslim who can afford to make it. The Hajj proper is made between the eighth and thirteenth days of the twelfth month of the Islamic calendar, and every pilgrim carries out specified rituals at particular times. At any other time of year, Muslims can perform similar prayers and rituals in Makkah (Mecca) and thus complete the "Umrah," or "lesser pilgrimage."

The Hajj season ends on the day of Eid-ul-Adha, the tenth day of the twelfth month of the Islamic lunar calendar.

Suggested discussion questions/activities:

    (i) Can you find Mecca/Saudi Arabia on the map?
    (ii) How could you get to Mecca from Canada?

(a) A pilgrim's journey is hard and difficult, so the maze is difficult. There are also different paths people take to get there so there is more than one way to solve the maze.

One maze solution

Figure 5.6. One Maze Solution

(b) Review assignment prior to the students completing it. The journey can be a trip to Disneyland or it can be going shopping with a special person.

Curricular Connections: Grade 1 Social Studies and Language Arts
In this particular activity teachers could ask the students to fill out a chart that is centered around a journey in which they are to contemplate the beginning, middle and end pieces. The teacher will ask the students to bring in an artifact from their trip that is important and

relevant. If they cannot bring in an artifact, ask them to bring in a photo of the artifact. Depending on the child's level of literacy, they may draw pictures, write short phrases or simple sentences to describe the beginning, middle and end.

Tell the children that today is a very special day because they are going to create their own classroom "museum." Display their written work alongside their artifact in the classroom "museum" and invite other classes to come and visit. Have the children stand beside their artifact in order to explain to their "visitors." You may want to have a child address the visiting class first to explain the project and why they are learning about the Muslim culture.

Activity: Comic Strip

Ages 5–6

Curriculum Connections: Grade 1 English Literacy

Illustrate the journey of a young Muslim child between two villages. Why would he/she be making this journey? What would it look like? Feel like? Smell like? And, what would they hear? Remember to think about who, what, where, when, why and how.

Activity: Story Writing

Ages 7–8

Curriculum Connections: Grade 2 English Literacy

Write and illustrate the journey of a young Muslim child between two villages. Why would he/she be making this journey? What would it look like? Feel like? Smell like? And, what would they hear? Remember to think about who, what, where, when, why and how. It is important to keep in mind that children need to visualize before they can begin to write. They will need lots of reference material and from that material they will need to create their own illustrations. Begin with the illustrations first so that they have a well-developed idea in mind.

Review the illustrations as a class and with peers for the correct and sufficient amount of detail. Are emotions properly depicted? How is distance between places and objects represented? The distance between people gives clues to the kind of relationship between them? Should there be trees? If there are trees, do they resemble the trees found in that region? This takes more time, but your students will have a deeper understanding.

Eid-ul-Adha

NOTE: The Hajj season ends on the day of Eid-ul-Adha, the tenth day of the twelfth month of the Islamic lunar calendar.

In 2007 Eid-ul-Adha was on or about December 20, and in 2008 it was about eleven days ahead, i.e., December 9.

Eid-ul-Adha is a festival day celebrated by Muslims to mark the end of Hajj season, and also to commemorate Ibrahim's (Abraham's) willingness to sacrifice his son Ismael (Ishmael).

Muslims on that day attend special congregational Eid prayers held in mosques or in large open areas (weather permitting), stadiums or arenas. They chant together, pray together, and the Imam offers a short sermon (khutba).

Worshipers greet and embrace each other after the congregational prayer; then they visit family and friends in the same city or in other cities and enjoy special meals made usually with lamb meat.

Class Discussion: Eid-ul-Adha
This Eid celebrates the Hajj pilgrimage. Muslims say special prayers. They feast with family and friends and they give meat to the poor. In many countries, the poor do not have meat because it is too expensive.

Activity: What is a pilgrimage?
Ages 7–8
Curricular Connections: Grade 2 Social Studies
How is the Muslim Hajj pilgrimage similar and different to the North American Aboriginal vision quest?

Class Discussion: Social Justice
Is Canada a great place to live? Why? What would make a person want to live in Canada? Remember to be mindful of a child's connection to their home. The planet is a beautiful place with lots to discover and

explore. We share this beautiful world we call home. Countries exist for a purpose and sometimes the people in charge make bad decisions. Entire countries and citizens are not bad, unfortunately a single persons decision, or a group of peoples decisions are strong enough to make a person have to leave. How can you celebrate and honor a Muslim child's culture, home and identity while at the same time poignantly explain why they may have had to leave their country.

Fiction books specific to Muslim children:
Four Feet, Two Sandals by Karen Lynn Williams and Khadar Mohammad
Listen to the Wind by Greg Mortenson
Malala Yousafzai: Warrior with Words by Karen Leggelt
Everyday is Malala's Day by Rosemary McCarney

Reading books about children around the world will broaden the children's worldview and help them understand the need to protect rights and freedoms as a global issue. Hopefully it will prevent the "us" and "them" scenario, as Canada too has been at fault. There are some great books for grade two based on the Inuit and Residential Schools. The objective is not to scare the children, dishearten them, or deflate patriotism, but instead to give them the information they can use when listening to the media or daily conversations. Education is power, and if we are going to mute racism and ignorance, we need to give children the information at an early age that allows them to build values and make sound opinions.

Fiction Books specific to children's freedoms around the world:
Henry's Freedom Box by Ellen Levine—Underground Railroad
Composition by Antonio Skarmeta—Chilean Dictatorship
A Day's Work by Eve Bunting—Mexican-American
Gleem and Glow by Eve Bunting—Civil War
Fatty Legs: A True Story by Christy Jordan-Fenton—Residential Schools (Inuit)
Not My Girl by Christy Jordan-Fenton—Residential Schools (Inuit)
When I Was Eight by Christy Jordan-Fenton—Residential Schools (Inuit)
A Stranger at Home: A True Story by Christy Jordan-Fenton—Residential Schools (Inuit)

I Have the Right to Be a Child by Alain Serres—UN Convention on the Rights of the Child

Grade 4: Islamic Art

1. Introduction to Islamic Buildings
Suggested discussion questions/activities:

> The mosque at Mecca
> (i) Locate Mecca on a map of the Middle East.
> (ii) Discuss why a journey to Mecca might be difficult.
> (iii) Explain that millions of people go there during the two weeks of hajj. Discuss what problems might occur with that many people arriving at the same time.

Inside a mosque

The students can draw lines from the word to the place in the mosque. They can circle the location. You can make an overhead transparency of the mosque and label it with the students.

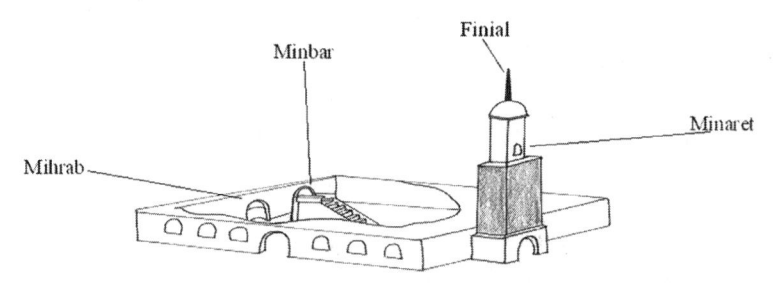

Figure 5.7. Label the Mosque

Discuss with the students difficult journeys they might have taken. It could be a car ride or an awful bus trip where they threw up.

Traditional décor at the mosque

The Alhambra in Granada, Spain is known for its beautiful decorative tiles. Have students color in a traditional tile such as the one below.

Possible coloring solution:

Figure 5.8. Colorful Tile

2. Carpets and Rugs
Recommended reading: D'Adamo, F. (D'Adamo, 2003). This true story is about children indentured to carpet factory owners in Pakistan.
  Suggested discussion questions/activities:

  (i) Discuss why people might have rugs/carpets in their houses.
  (ii) How do people pick colors and designs?

NOTE Prayer rugs: usually can see a top and a bottom to the rugs. The top is always placed in the direction of Mecca.

Introduction
Rugs are traditionally created using a loom. Discuss the following topics with the students. See website http://islamicart.com/main/rugs/intro.html

1. The height of the loom. There are three weavers.
2. Turkish Knot. Persian Knot.
3. Knotted fringe, Machine-made fringe.

Weaving and knotting
1. The loom is on the ground. The weaver is sitting on the rug, on the loom.
2. The loom is on the wall. The weaver is sitting in front of the loom.
3. Weaving with the loom on the wall would be a more comfortable way to weave.

Designing a rug
Perhaps have students speak about their designs: why they chose the lines, shapes, etc., and colors that they did—post the designs for others to see.

3. Calligraphy

Class Discussion: Islamic Architecture

Geometric patterns and arabesques have developed over the centuries in Islamic decoration. Arabesques are linear patterns of scrolling and interlacing foliage, tendrils or plain lines. To Muslims arabesques are ongoing and symbolize the nature of creation by Allah and the Islamic Worldview. Islamic art does not have the figurative iconography that other religions do and in fact it is not permitted to recreate living forms because that is considered the work of God. There are two types of Islamic decoration: In the first type each repeating geometric form has a built-in symbolism ascribed to it. The second type is based upon the flowing nature of plant forms. Some argue that Arabic calligraphy is a third type of arabesque art.

Suggested discussion questions/activities:
(i) If possible, invite a calligrapher to come to the class and give a demonstration of how to use calligraphy pens. It may be possible for the school to get a set of inexpensive, disposable calligraphy pens for the students to use for this activity.
(ii) Ask the students where they have seen calligraphy used. Why do people use calligraphy?

FOUNDATIONS FOR AN ANTI-ISLAMOPHOBIC CURRICULUM 111

- (iii) Have you seen calligraphy used as art? Where?
- (iv) Prior to the students completing the exercise, have them try writing a sentence from left to right in English.

NOTE: Arabic letter workbooks are available at http://islamicbookstore.com/
In the same way that Islamic pottery is decorated using Arabic script, try and decorate this jug using English script.

Possible solution to jug design:

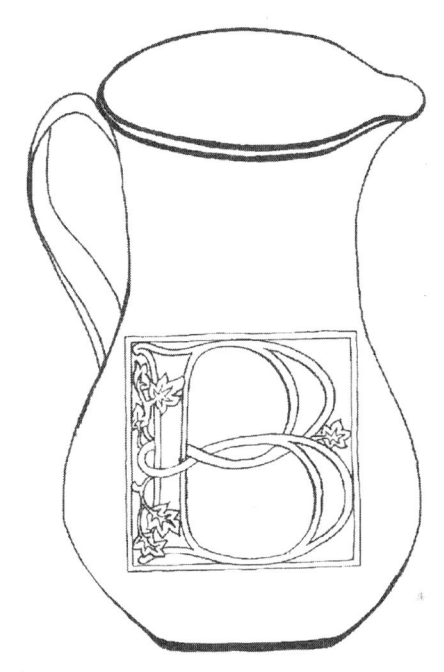

Figure 5.9. Calligraphy Jug

4. Headdresses, Jewelry, and Perfume
Suggested discussion activities/activities:

- (i) If possible, bring in a number of different head coverings—perhaps some are available at the school's lost and found—and discuss who would wear them and why they would wear them.
- (ii) What influences what we wear on our head?
- (iii) Do people in Canada wear different head coverings in different regions? Explain why.

Headdresses

1. <u>False</u>—Muslims wear different types of head covering depending on age, social status, marriage status, ethnic group, etc.
2. <u>True</u>—Some head coverings are works of art.
3. <u>False</u>—The climate of the region affects what Muslims wear.
4. <u>False</u>—A married person does not wear the same type of head covering as an unmarried person.
5. <u>True</u>—The type of head covering a Muslim wears may differ depending on social status.

Jewelry

Suggested discussion activities:

(i) What kind of jewelry might people in this class wear?
(ii) What limits the jewelry that you wear?
(iii) What kind of jewelry do you think you should wear?

Perfume

Suggested discussion activities:

(i) Bring in store samples of perfume for the students to smell. Check for allergies prior to doing this activity.
- students can select the perfume they like the best/worst
- students can check the ingredients to see what the perfume is made from and how ingredients differ from one perfume to the next

(ii) Why do you think people wear perfume?
(iii) Can you think of why perfume might have been invented?

Group Project

Possible solutions:

Basic steps to making perfume:

Collection

- Flowers, spices, fruits, wood, leaves and animal products are collected. These can be used in any combination or on their own.

Extraction
- Oil is extracted from scent base using various methods of extraction including steam distillation.

Blending
- Between five percent and ten percent oil is blended with eighty percent alcohol and ten percent water.

Aging
- Perfume is bottled and aged for several months or years.

To make your own perfume:

Materials:
Cotton pads
Funnel
Pipettes
Measuring Cup
Measuring Spoon
Plastic or Glass Bottle

Essential oil (any scent you desire)	five drops
Grain Alcohol (vodka)	one-fourth cup
Spring Water	two tbsp
Glycerine	one tbsp

Method:
Mix together the oil and alcohol. Let the mixture sit for forty-eighty hours or longer. When the desired scent is achieved, add the spring water and the glycerin. Test the scent on a cotton pad. Add additional water if the scent is too strong. Store in a glass or plastic container.

Figure 5.10. Examples of Perfume Bottles

Final Activity

In this activity students are asked to engage in an internet scavenger hunt in which they are given six questions related to the Taj Mahal. Questions include:

1. What is the Taj Mahal?
2. Where is it located?
3. What is cartouche?
4. What could cartouche be used for in an Islamic building?
5. Where is the Dome of the rock?
6. What is the Dome of the rock?

Answers to the internet scavenger hunt:

1. A monument/mausoleum
2. India
3. An oval shaped named plaque usually written in hieroglyphics
4. To name the builder of the building or dedication of the building
5. Jerusalem
6. Islamic Shrine

Introduction to Islamic Heritage

The legacy of Islamic scholars and inventors goes back over 1000 years. There are four areas that will be investigated: botany, mathematics, irrigation, and geography. However, there are many areas like medicine, architecture, and law that have strong and important legacies as well.

1. Botany

As the Islamic world grew, Muslims began to settle from Spain to China. They were able to grow and cultivate even the driest lands. They could identify what plants would grow in certain soils and they mastered grafting techniques. Grafting is the method of attaching a piece of one plant to another. The two pieces join and become one plant. People who were skilled at grafting could take plants from one area and introduce them to another area.

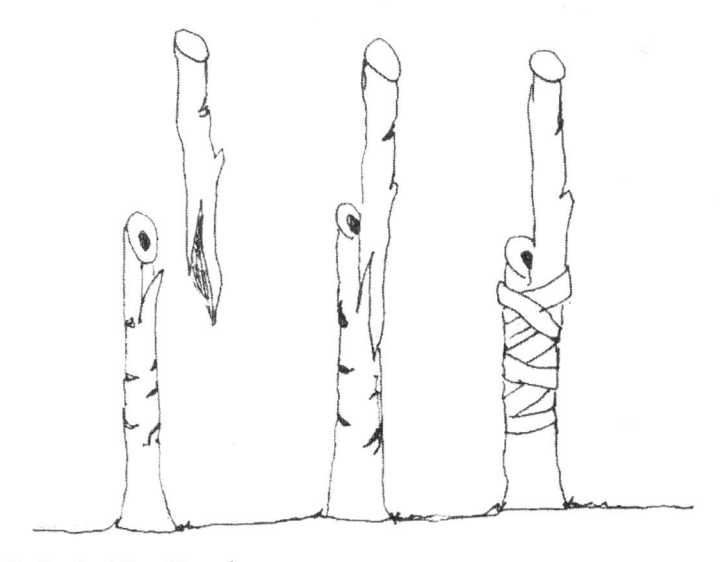

Figure 5.11. Grafted Tree Branches

Hundreds of years before Linnaeus created the Western system of plant **classification**, Ibn Baytar or Ibn Baitar (1197–1248 CE) developed a classification system for plants that was well known and highly regarded in the Islamic world. Ibn Baytar was interested in **pharmaceutical** herbs and flowers. He explored throughout Spain and Morocco, looking for new and unique **medicinal** herbs and flowers. He created a dictionary of 2000 herbs and flowers, explaining what they were and how they could be used. He wrote the information in Arabic, Greek, **Berber**, Latin, as well as in several local **dialects**. He wanted everyone to have this knowledge.

(i) Find the meaning that best suits each of the bolded words in the paragraph.
   (a) classification
   (b) pharmaceutical
   (c) medicinal
   (d) Berber
   (e) dialects
(ii) Logical groups

Add as many lines as needed.
1. _____, _____, _____

because _____.

2. _____, _____, _____

because _____.

3. _____, _____, _____

because _____.

2. Mathematics

Islamic mathematicians laid the foundations for modern mathematics. They gathered information from Indian and Greek mathematicians. To this information, they added their own knowledge.

Al-Khwarizmi (780–850 CE) was one of the first mathematical faculty members at the Dar al – Hikma or House of Wisdom in Baghdad.

FOUNDATIONS FOR AN ANTI-ISLAMOPHOBIC CURRICULUM

The House of Wisdom was dedicated to the promotion of teaching and learning.

Al-Khwarizmi wrote two mathematical text books which played an important role in the history of math. The first book contained the Arab word al-jabr in its title. Its content dealt with the development of solutions to mathematical problems in which there was an unknown quantity. He wanted the book to be practical so people could use it to measure their lands and dig their canals.

$$\text{Examples: } a = l \times w \qquad v = l \times w \times h$$

Western monks transliterated the title into Latin. They spelled the word using the characters of the Latin alphabet. It became algebra.

His second book introduced the Hindu numbering system. Scholars soon found the nine characters, 1, 2, 3, 4, 5, 6, 7, 8, 9, and the use of the circle for zero far superior to the Roman numerals they had been using.

Scholars had been able to add and subtract Roman numerals but were unable to do anything more complicated. Because the Europeans learned this system from the Arabs, it has been referred to as the Arabic numbering system even though it was originally developed by Hindus.

There are seven letters that represent all Roman numerals. They can be used alone or in various combinations to make every number.

This chart shows how the numbering system changed.

(a) Write the following using Roman numerals.

    Your birth year   _____

    The year your house was built   _____

    The current Super Bowl   _____

    Chapter 45   _____

    The year your school was built   _____

(b) Fill in the chart.

XXX	
	97
	53
XC	
MMVIII	
XLVI	
	160
	7000
LM	
	555

Figure 5.12. Roman Numerals Chart

(c) Answer the following problems.

L – XV = _____

CL + V = _____

M – DL = _____

(d) Why do you think Arab scholars dropped Roman numerals and began using the Hindu system?
(e) Why do you think people use Roman numerals today?
(f) What effect do you think the development of zero (0) has had on mathematics?

3. Irrigation

As the Islamic world grew, so did their influence on agriculture. They had extensive botanical resources but many needed a regular supply of water. So, in order to grow bananas, sugar cane, and coffee, they developed a widespread irrigation system.

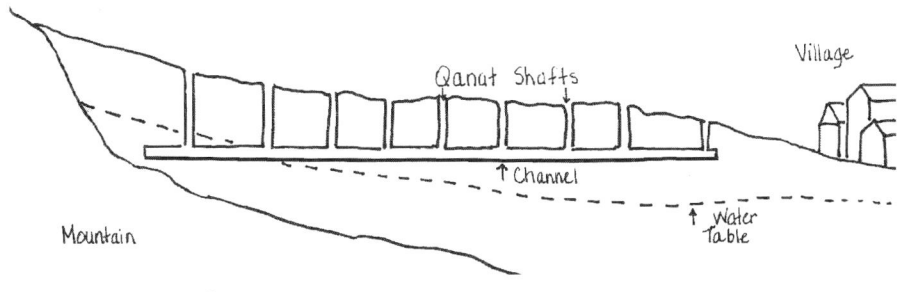

Figure 5.13. Qanat System

In some places, qanats were built. These were tunnels that carried water from an underground source to a ground surface in another location. In Iran, there are 274,000 kilometers of underground channels. Until a few years ago, most of the network was still working, over a thousand years after they were first built.

Norias, similar to water wheels, were also constructed to provide an ongoing water supply to agricultural lands. They provided water everywhere.

Muslims also developed canal networks which supplied the water necessary for the production of crops, particularly in Spain. Many canals continue to provide water to orchards and rice fields today.

Use this website to see how canalling worked in Mesopotamia, the area now known as Iraq, parts of Syria and Turkey and southwest Iran.

http://www.mesopotamia.co.uk/geography/challenge/cha_set.html

Today, environmentalists hold these traditional methods of irrigation in high esteem. Edward Goldsmith, an environmentalist, writes:

> Modern irrigation schemes in tropical areas are **almost without exception**, social, ecological and economic disasters. They necessarily lead to the flooding of vast areas of forest and agricultural land, the **displacement** of hundreds of thousands of people and the spreading of waterborne diseases like **malaria** and **schistosomiasis**. In addition, they are badly run, poorly maintained and the irrigated land is soon **salinized** or water-logged, while the reservoirs where the water is stored, rapidly **silt** up. The remarkable traditional irrigation systems they have replaced, on the other hand, not only worked perfectly, but also satisfied all social and ecological **imperatives**.

Rather than the simpler qanats and norias of the past, governments have encouraged the construction of dams as a relatively cheap way of providing water for irrigation and hydro power for generating electricity.

Because of advances in concrete technology and the invention of machines that can literally move mountains, today's dams are huge. But they come at a cost. China's Three Gorges dam on the Yangtze River has caused 1.2 million people to relocate.

(a) Explain the following words as they apply to the reading.
   (i) almost without exception
   (ii) displacement
   (iii) malaria
   (iv) schistosomiasis
   (v) salinized
   (vi) silt
   (v) imperatives
(b) Why do you think countries build huge dams to supply irrigation needs rather than relying on traditional Islamic methods?
(c) Debate: Traditional Islamic methods of irrigation have a place in today's environment.

Students learn about wetland ecosystems by studying life in a local pond, slough, marsh, fen or bog. Through classroom studies, and studies in the field, students learn about organisms that live in, on and around wetlands and about adaptations that suit pond organisms to their environment. Through observation and research, students learn

about the interactions among wetland organisms and about the role of each organism as part of a food web. The role of human action in affecting wetland habitats and populations is also studied.
Wetland Ecosystem

GENERAL OUTCOME

Students will describe the living and nonliving components of a wetland ecosystem and the interactions within and among them.

KNOWLEDGE AND UNDERSTANDING

Students will:
Recognize and describe one or more examples of wetland ecosystems found in the local area; e.g., pond, slough, marsh, bog, fen.
Understand that a wetland ecosystem involves interactions between living and nonliving things, both in and around the water.
Identify some plants and animals found at a wetland site, both in and around the water; and describe the life cycles of these plants and animals.
Identify and describe adaptations that make certain plants and animals suited for life in a wetland.
Understand and appreciate that all animals and plants, not just the large ones, have an important role in a wetland community.
Identify the roles of different organisms in the food web of a pond:
Producers—green plants that make their own food, using sunlight
Consumers—animals that eat living plants and/or animals
Decomposers—organisms, such as molds, fungi, insects and worms, that reuse and recycle materials that were formerly living.
Draw diagrams of food chains and food webs, and interpret such diagrams.
Recognize that some aquatic animals use oxygen from air and others from water, and identify examples and adaptations of each.
Identify human actions that can threaten the abundance or survival of living things in wetland ecosystems; e.g., adding pollutants, changing the flow of water, trapping or hunting pond wildlife.
Identify individual and group actions that can be taken to preserve and enhance wetland habitats.

Recognize that changes in part of an environment have effects on the whole environment.
Physical Geography of Canada

GENERAL OUTCOME

Students will demonstrate an understanding and appreciation of how the physical geography and natural resources of Canada affect the quality of life of all Canadians.

VALUES AND ATTITUDES

Students will:
Value Canada's physical geography and natural environment:
Appreciate the variety and abundance of natural resources in Canada.
Appreciate the diversity of geographic phenomena in Canada.
Appreciate the environmental significance of national parks and protected areas in Canada.
Appreciate how the land sustains communities and the diverse ways that people have of living with the land.
Appreciate the influence of the natural environment on the growth and development of Canada.
Demonstrate care and concern for the environment through their choices and actions.
Appreciate the geographic vastness of Canada.

KNOWLEDGE AND UNDERSTANDING

Students will:
Examine, critically, the physical geography of Canada by exploring and reflecting upon the following questions and issues: What are the major geographical regions, landforms and bodies of water in Canada?
How do landforms, bodies of water and natural resources affect the quality of life in Canada?
What are the differences and similarities among the geographical regions of Canada?

How is the geographical region they live in different from other regions of Canada?
What are the factors that determine climate in the diverse geographical regions of Canada (e.g., latitude, water, mountains)?
How are Canada's national parks and protected areas important to the sustainability of Canada's natural environment?

Analyze how people in Canada interact with the environment by exploring and reflecting upon the following questions and issues:
In what ways do natural resources and the physical geography of a region determine the establishment of communities?
How are natural resources used, exchanged and conserved in Canada?
Whose responsibility should it be to ensure the preservation of Canada's national parks and protected areas?
Social studies kindergarten to Grade 12. (Alberta Education, 2005)

Lessons and Activities:
Class Discussion: Dams
As students have learned, dams today can be harmful to the environment, whereas the older forms of irrigation where not. In Grade 5 students learn about the Alberta wetlands and the preservation of those lands. How can the development of a dam be harmful to Alberta wetlands?
Activity: Compare and Contrast

Curricular Connections: Grade 5 Science
Compare and contrast the irrigation systems of early Islamic communities: example the Moors in Spain and the Mezquita in Cordoba; to the construction of a dam in Alberta: example the Glenmore Reservoir in Calgary.

PART ONE: Photo Essay
Create a photo essay using Blogger, Exposure or another Web 2.0 platform where you can showcase your work.
https://www.blogger.com
https://exposure.co
Using photos you have taken and those from your research, you will tell a story with images that will evoke a response from your audience.

PART TWO: Vidcast

Using Seesaw, Shadow Puppet Edu, or any other Web 2.0 tool, you will create a vidcast. This means you will add audio to your selection of powerful images. For examples of other student work go to http://getpuppet.co/#classroomStoriesShort. For this activity you will need an iPad.
http://get-puppet.co
http://web.seesaw.me

Videos:

National Geographic: http://natgeotv.com/ca/ancientmegastructures/Videos/petra-water-in-the-desert
Resources: Engineering

Hagia Sofia: Dome Secrets

National Geographic: http://natgeotv.com/ca/ancientmegastructures/videos/hagia-sofia-dome-secrets
Class Discussion: Guest Speaker
The teacher could ask the student's parents if any of them are engineers, historians, natives to the area being studied, or have visited the area and sites. The guest could come in and speak to the children about their knowledge and understanding of the mathematics behind the construction of such buildings, or they could show pictures and talk about their experiences bring life to the topic.
Activity: Build a Palace

Curricular Connections: Grade 5 Math and Science

As you have learned, the Muslims were at the forefront of the development of mathematical concepts such as geometry, algebra, and numeracy. All of these things are necessary for an engineer. Imagine you have been hired to build a palace for a Sultan. You will need to think about:

- The number of rooms
- Walls
- Doors and entry ways
- Windows
- Pathways
- Patios
- Gardens

- Water – fountains, pools, irrigation system
- Throne room
- Religious rooms
- Entertainment and dining rooms
- Baths
- Research what other components made up a palace.

Create a birds-eye view of the palace and then chose three rooms to draw in detail. Then scan your drawings, or take a steady photo, and upload them to your blog. Finish your project by writing about your ideas, reasoning, and inspirations. Connect your showcase of learning to specific information you learned in class by referring to them in your writing.

References

Alberta Education. (2005). Social studies kindergarten to grade 12. https://education.alberta.ca/media/773693/ss5.pdf

Alberta Education. (2015). Social studies: Program of studies. http://www.education.alberta.ca/teachers/program/socialstudies/programs/

D'Adamo, F. (2003). *Iqbal* (A. Leonon, Trans.). New York, NY: Atheneum Books for Young Readers.

Global Living Global Learning. (2015). Living together: Muslims in a changing world. http://www.living-together.ca/

Luke, A. (2005). Evidence-based state literacy policy: A critical alternative. In Bascia, N., Cumming, A., Datnow, A., Leithwood, K., & Livingstone, D. (Eds.), *International Handbook of Educational Policy*. Great Britain: Springer.

Naqvi, R. (2008). Living together: Muslims in a changing world, curriculum series. http://www.living-together.ca/index.shtml

National Geographic. (2013). Petra: water in the desert. [Webpage]. Retrieved from http://natgeotv.com/ca/ancientmegastructures/Videos/petra-water-in-the-desert

Smith, D. G. (2008). Preface: Living together, learning together. http://www.living-together.ca/pdfs/teachersguide.pdf

Wallace, J. (May 26, 2014). Canada's four models of religion-state relations. Retrieved from http://www.davidanderson.ca/canadas-four-models-of-religion-state-relations/

Wilkinson, P. (2002). *Islam*. New York, NY: Dorling Kindersley.

Zia, F. (2013). *The garden of Imaan*. Atlanta, GA: Peachtree Publishers.

Zine, J. (2004). Anti-Islamophobia education as transformative pedagogy: Reflections from the educational frontlines. *American Journal of Islamic Social Sciences, Special Issue: Orientalism, Neo-Orientalism and Islamophobia, 21*(3), 110–120.

Conclusion

"At school the politics of identity have changed because of 9/11. Ethnicity and culture used to be curiosities. Now, while diversity is still celebrated, there is a new recognition that ethnicity can be an undesirable element of one's identity."
(Gardner, 2003, para. 9)

"The events of 9/11 exploded the myth of "us" and "them" or "here" and "there." Foreign war and political upheaval are not far-away things because they have a direct link to a young person sitting in my classroom. Globalization has brought us together in a strange place: a small classroom in Western Canada."
(Gardner, 2003, para. 13)

"Grass roots engagement will build trust, provide awareness of risks and vulnerabilities, educate partners about resources available to assist individuals at risk and enhance the shared responsibility."
(Calgary Herald, 2014, para. 22)

The Canadian Multiculturalism Act was the legislative guarantee and precedent that allowed for more attention being paid to increased diversity in the education system. This stipulated, the "Government of Canada recognizes the diversity of Canadians as regards race, national or ethnic origin, colour and religion as a fundamental characteristic of Canadian society and is committed to a policy of multiculturalism designed to preserve and enhance the multicultural heritage of Canadians while working to achieve the equality of all Canadians in the economic, social, cultural and political life of Canada."

(Government of Canada, 2015, para, 8)

"Internationally recognized peace educator, Johan Galtung, once remarked that 'there can be no peace in the world without peace among the world's religions.' Such words seem especially relevant today when so many conflicts around the world are being cast as religious conflicts, conflicts over fundamental human values. It is not the place here to engage this debate except perhaps to note a growing generalized dissatisfaction with values that are purely materialistic. People everywhere are expressing a need to link the joys and burdens of life to something more than material production and accumulation. Life needs to be experienced as something 'holy', a word derived from the Old English 'hal' meaning 'whole'."

(Smith, 2008, para. 1)

As a teacher preparation tool or a living document within the practicing teacher's toolkit, this book has presented an historical perspective of phobia, with a focus on current issues relating to the sociophobic reactions towards the Muslim culture. One cannot underestimate the importance and global scale of this occurrence and placing a potential solution to the problem within the realm of education is one step in the right direction. All teacher education programs now include modules on diversity and include discussions around educators' own history, culture, biases, opinions, and experiences.

Nevertheless, the historical trajectory outlined in the initial chapters of this book demonstrates how exercising culturally responsive pedagogy alone is no longer a viable strategy that can effectively address the issue of sociophobic reaction. Today, we are dealing with a type of tension in our society that needs to be examined through a different lens, focusing on a knowledgeable framework that helps us better understand what we are dealing with. This involves working towards a sustainable framework of cultural integration between education and society. This book has proposed a positive model, which brings together a basic knowledge of an immigrant group with the goal of recognizing the essential building blocks of a progressive society: The recognition of individual multiculturality, cultural diversity, and contributions to society.

Writing this book and thinking about the historical trajectory of events that have precipitated its publishing, I am led in my own mind to ask two questions:

So What?

It is no doubt inevitable that in today's classroom any teacher, at any given time, will have students who are from diverse backgrounds (e.g., Muslim) and will be working to build community in their classroom and school. It is important that work be done toward eliminating stereotypes and helping to reduce phobic reactions towards cultural groups in the school and larger community.

I believe that the approaches proposed in this book will go a long way toward helping educators address the cultural realities of the world today and create in their classroom an opportunity to capitalize on the diversity and wonderful richness that comes with this reality and build on an already well-thought-out curriculum. This book has attempted to address this in a practical, user-friendly manner that allows a certain amount of flexibility to move the activities around and use them in different contexts and with other cultures.

Where Do We Go From Here?

This book has clearly demonstrated the rise of phobic reaction and its strong relationship with terrorism. Canada is not alone in wanting its education system to include antiphobic curricula. The United States and much of Europe has also expressed interest in moving forward to try and thwart the increasing sociophobic reaction to immigrant groups. Such an approach involves using History and Social Studies education in an effort to build and deepen democratic societies, linking professionals around the world, ethnicities and religions. An antiphobic curriculum seeks to build capacity for educators, helping education programs and schools to produce and implement innovative teaching tools. It provides an innovative, easily integrated approach to combatting societal phobias through systemic work at the grass roots level beginning as early as grade 1 and works hand in hand with the current curricular objectives of critical thinking, mutual respect, peace, stability, and democracy.

The European Union, in its desire to squelch the rising paranoia resulting from terrorism and increasing movement towards radicalization (especially among its youth|), has already taken steps within its educational systems. Educators currently have access to resources such as:

- Erasmus: A program that recognizes that technologies are changing the way society operates and there is a need to ensure the best use is made of them. Erasmus recognizes the need for the EU to become more competitive through talent and innovation. It hopes to provide young people with the skills required by the labor market and the new economy and allow them to play an active role in society and achieve personal fulfillment. Particular attention is paid to immigrants. Its desire is to ensure contributions to growth and prosperity and social inclusion in Europe and beyond. (EC.Europa.EU)
- Sirius: is a European policy network on the education of children with a migrant background. Its primary objective is to improve educational measures for migrant students ensuring they can raise their educational standards and outcomes to at least that of majority groups.
- EUROCLIO, the European Association of History Educators: supports the development of responsible and innovative history, citizenship and heritage education as a way to promote critical thinking, mutual respect, peace, stability and democracy. The Association advocates a sound use of history and heritage education towards the building and deepening of democratic societies, connecting professionals across boundaries of countries, ethnicities and religions. It seeks to enhance the quality of history and citizenship education through capacity building for educators and producing and implementing innovative teaching tools (Benarab-Attou & Valjalo, 2013).

The ideas developed within this book build on what is currently in place and have global application for any educational endeavors and can be easily connected with current initiatives being undertaken similar to those described above. In fact, this book presents a practical, unifying agenda that facilitates smooth transitions between it and any other resources.

Nevertheless, in spite of all the initiatives and programs being undertaken around the world, we are still not at the point where we can say all is well. Our reaction to people who are different from us continues to be fodder for discussion and reactive movements such as radicalization. Wilner and Dubouloz (2010) define radicalization "as a process by which an individual or group comes to adopt increasingly extreme political, social or religious ideals or aspirations that reject or undermine the status quo." Issues of identity have long been recognized as being central to radicalization and are not unique to Muslims. The radicalization movement has created an even more prevalent sociophobic reaction worldwide, making the case for grass root level movements such as this curriculum even more urgent as we continue to chip away at seeking to understand all the grievances and myriad individual triggers that might drive an individual to join an extremist group. Addressing the issue of identity is difficult and contentious and needs to be borne out of a sense of shared belonging where each individual sees him or herself as a part of a unified history and a social being, contributing to the collective wellbeing of society.

I end this book in the hope that educators, students and education programs alike will be able to benefit from its pages; deepening their understanding of the wonderful opportunities that lie in learning from each other.

References

Benarab-Attou , M., & Valjalo, O. (2013). Teaching history for democratic citizenship: How does history education contribute to social cohesion and respect for diversity today? *Proceedings of the 3rd EUCIS-LLL Lifelong Learning Week and the NEPC Project Making History for Tolerance: A Research Based Strategy to Reduce the Intolerant Usage of*

History Teaching in the EU. Retrieved from http://www.sirius-migrationeducation.org/wp-content/uploads/2013/10/NEPC_Teaching_History_Event_BRU.pdf

Calgary Herald. (2014, August 30). Islamic radicalization of Canadian youth raises alarm bells. Retrieved from http://calgaryherald.com/news/local-news/islamic-radicalization-of-canadian-youth-raises-alarm-bells.

Gardner, R. (2003). Teaching after 9/11. *Canadian Social Studies, 38*(1). Retrieved from http://www2.education.ualberta.ca/css/Css_38_1/ARteaching_after 9_11.htm

Government of Canada. (2015, July 10). Canadian Multiculturalism Act R.S.C., 1985, c. 24 (4th Supp.). Retrieved from http://laws-lois.justice.gc.ca/eng/acts/C-18.7/FullText.html

Smith, D. G. (2008). Preface: Living together, learning together. Retrieved from http://www.living-together.ca/pdfs/teachersguide.pdf

Wilner, A., & Dubouloz, C.-J. (2010). Homegrown terrorism and transformative learning: An interdisciplinary approach to understanding radicalization. *Global Change, Peace, & Security, 22*(1), 35–51.

CPC
CRITICAL PRAXIS AND CURRICULUM GUIDES

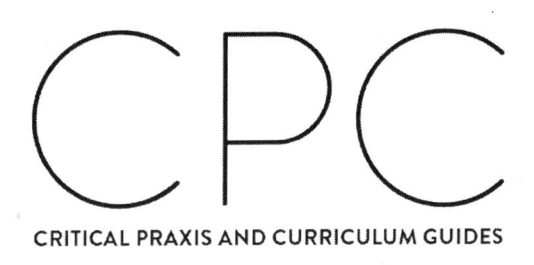

Shirley R. Steinberg and Priya Parmar
Series Editors

Critical Praxis and Curriculum Guides is a curriculum-based book series reflective of theory-creating praxis. The series targets not only undergraduate and graduate audiences but also tenured and experienced teachers of all disciplines. Research suggests that teachers need well-designed, thematic-centered curricula and lessons. This is accomplished when the school works as a community to meet its own needs. Community in this sense includes working collaboratively with students, parents, and local community organizations to help build the curriculum. Practically, this means that time is devoted to professional development workshops, not exam reviews or test preparation pointers but real learning. Together with administrators, teachers form professional learning communities (PLCs) to discuss, analyze, and revise curricula and share pedagogical strategies that meet the needs of their particular school demographics. This communal approach was found to be more successful than requiring each individual teacher to create lessons on her/his own. Ideally, we would love it if each teacher could create his/her own authentic lessons because only s/he truly knows her/his students—and we encourage it, because it is possible! However, as educators ourselves, we understand the realities our colleagues in public schools face, especially when teaching in high-needs areas.

The Critical Praxis and Curriculum Guides series provides relief for educators needing assistance in preparing their lessons. In the spirit of communal practices, the series welcomes co-authored books by theorists and practitioners as well as solo-authored books by an expert deeply informed by the field. Because we strongly believe that theory guides our practice, each guide will blend theory and curriculum chapters, creating a praxis—all, of course, in a critical pedagogical framework. The guides will serve as resources for teachers to use, expand upon, revise, and re-create.

For additional information about this series or for the submission of manuscripts, please contact either Shirley R. Steinberg at msgramsci@aol.com or Priya Parmar at priyaparmar_24@hotmail.com. To order other books in this series, please contact our Customer Service Department: (800) 770-LANG (within the U.S.); (212) 647-7706 (outside the U.S.); (212) 647-7707 FAX; or browse online by series at www.peterlang.com.